Testimon

'My friend Matt Bird is a consum
relationship expert. This very practical book gives you tne
"tips of his trade" – including how he changed from
cowering behind the sofa to hobnobbing with the PM.
Highly recommended.'
Jeremy Marshall, CEO of C. Hoare & Co Bank

'If you're in the business of winning business read this book!'
Sir Peter Vardy, Chair of the Vardy Group

'Relevant, authentic and innovative – *Relationology* is a "must"
for anyone seeking to properly develop their contacts.'
Alex Fox, Head of IP at Penningtons Manches LLP

'All businesses are focused on growth. If you have personal
responsibility for winning, keeping or growing new business
then you need to read this book, focused on practical things
you can do.'
Richard Oldfield, Executive Board at PwC

'Don't underestimate the power of your network, it is
connecting with interesting people and building meaningful
relationships that gives you the competitive edge. This book
shows you how.'
**Gemma Greaves, Managing Director of The
Marketing Society**

'To build business relationships, you need to understand
them. Matt's book is the authority on doing just that.'
Helen Weisinger, Marketing Partner at Portas Agency

'Connecting with people is key to a happy and fulfilling life. Matt's book provides an uncomplicated but insightful route map toward success.'
Nigel Holland, Regional President EMEA of Tata Global Beverages

'The business of new business boils down to one thing: the impact you make with your prospective clients. This book has everything you need to make sure your business is the most memorable on the pitch list.'
Cormac Loughran, Chief Marketing Officer at Dentsu Aegis Network

'Matt has made the business of networking his domain and this excellent toolkit will help you benefit from his invaluable skills.'
Neil Robinson, Digital Director of IPC Media, A Time Warner Company

'Incredibly useful, practical and astute, Matt Bird's advice and tips on building better relationships are an insightful read. It's the sort of book that you need to read again and again.'
Nick Ashley, Chief Client Officer at Mindshare

'If you are involved in new business development and client relationship management then *Relationology* is a must read and helped me hugely.'
Lady Natasha Rufus Isaac, Co-Founder of Beulah

'*Relationology* is a much-needed book on how to achieve better business relationships, and the significant impact they can have. I would recommend it to anyone seeking practical

advice on improving the way in which they relate to others in the business world.'
Gary Streeter MP

'For many professions and institutions, we are living in an age of lost trust. The ideas that Matt Bird expresses in *Relationology* will not only help you be more effective in your relationships, but will allow you to do so with integrity.'
David Savage, Head of Property Services at Charles Russell LLP

'This book is filled with ideas that are both wise and very practical. If you follow Matt's advice you will build better relationships both at work and at play.'
Simon Pilcher, CEO of Fixed Income at M&G Investments

'If you struggle with "networking" then you will love Relationology!'
Rob Parsons, Author of The Heart of Success

'If you aspire to be an exceptional trusted adviser Matt Bird's book is a must read.'
Nana Yaw Oduro, Chair of First Allied Bank

'Matt Bird's secrets for building better business relationships are inspiring and immensely practical.'
Kelle Bryan, CEO of Red Hot Entertainment

'Simple and practical read. Powerful if applied.'
Ben Collins, Managing Director of Stephen James BMW

'Relationships sit at the heart of any business – indeed any life. Matt's "secrets" are short, pithy – and inspiring; there is real wisdom in these pages – enjoy!'
Major General Tim Cross CBE

'The *Relationology* approach developed by Matt Bird is hugely insightful and is a must for encouraging effectiveness.'
Professor Nigel Sykes, Warwick Business School

'In tough times, money always flows through the strongest connections. Matt Bird knows this and gives us the power to harness our connections. A brilliant book for all business people!'
Rob Brown, Founder of the Networking Coaching Academy

'If ever there was a definitive reference guide on how to build strong mutually beneficial relationships, then this book is it.'
Heather Townsend, Author of *The FT Guide to Business Networking*

Relationology™

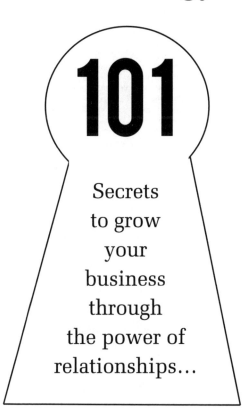

101

Secrets
to grow
your
business
through
the power of
relationships...

Matt Bird

Matador
9 Priory Business Park
Kibworth Beauchamp
Leicestershire LE8 0RX, UK
Tel: (+44) 116 279 2299
Fax: (+44) 116 279 2277
Email: books@troubador.co.uk
Web: www.troubador.co.uk/matador

ISBN 978 1783064 779 (Paperback)
9781 783064 786 (Hardback)

British Library Cataloguing in Publication Data.
A catalogue record for this book is available from the British Library.

Typeset by Troubador Publishing Ltd, Leicester, UK
Printed and bound in the UK by TJ International, Padstow, Cornwall

Matador is an imprint of Troubador Publishing Ltd

Dedicated to my wife Esther and our
three children Joseph, Matilda and Reuben

Contents

Turning a stranger into a "friend"

Secure an initial meeting

Overcoming self-doubt

Part B: Keep Relationships

Keeping your relationships alive

Part C: Grow Relationships

Growing relationships

Shifting a relationship that's become stale

Building your business through referral relationships

Becoming an exceptional trusted adviser

Introduction

Most school day afternoons from my childhood were the same. I'd come home, snack, play and attempt to play amicably with my sister. When my dad arrived home, freshened himself up, flopped onto the sofa and flicked on the TV, it was my cue to play a little more quietly and cease my negotiations. Dad liked to keep the house to himself. That's just how things were, and I didn't even question the times when, on hearing the doorbell ring, Dad would mute the TV and usher my mum, sister and I to hide behind the sofa, pretending no one was home.

It took a decade or two to realise that normal, sociable families do not hide behind the sofa when someone rings the doorbell. It took a little longer to work out that my father's way of looking at – and responding to – the world had a big impact on me. I grew up without an understanding that relationships were important and I developed a distinct lack of relational confidence. Gradually, I began to see how different my upbringing was to other people's. Reading biographies of prominent figures in public life showed me that being brought up within a sociable family environment can nurture incredible relational confidence, and it did not take long before I began to want to change the way I was. Having finally recognised what was missing from my own childhood I made a commitment to invest in relationships.

I'm a relationship geek. I'm fascinated by the way they shape us, and I'm constantly on the hunt for greater insight and wisdom into the way they work. Of course, I'm still an avid reader, but I have also had the privilege of building relationships with some of the very people these books are written about. From Business CEOs and government ministers to international figures and celebrities, I have been able to see up close what it means to have highly developed relational skills.

It has become clear to me that those who have succeeded in both public life and the business world have one thing in common – relationships. Each of them had someone who knew, liked and trusted them enough to want to help. Eventually this gave them an unprecedented opportunity which accelerated or changed their trajectory to greater life significance and business success. In other words, being known, liked and trusted by the right people transforms your life prospects and possibilities.

The true currency of business is not money; it is relationships. As Franklin D Roosevelt once said, 'The most important single ingredient in the formula of success is knowing how to get along with people'. More than any other factor it is the quality of your relationships that drive the bottom line of your life significance and business success. People choose to do business with people they know, like and trust. Time and time again I hear about contracts worth hundreds of thousands and tens of millions of pounds in which the character and history of the supplier are absolutely vital considerations. If you're looking for the ultimate competitive advantage and market differentiator, look no further than the way you relate to people.

By the time I was old enough to file a tax return, I'd worked out that I never wanted to hide behind the sofa. I'd discovered a better way of living and a greater source of inspiration, connection and satisfaction than I could ever have imagined. I embarked upon a journey to discover all that I could about the way we connect with other people, to get better at it myself and help others to do the same.

I didn't know it at the time, but my journey really began when I received an invitation to speak at a business conference. 'Sure,' I said. 'What do you want me to speak on?'

'Networking,' they told me. I cringed. It might seem odd to you, but I – like so many other people – have an absolute aversion to networking.

At its worst, networking is self-serving, shallow and short-term. Networking sees relationships as a means to an end and not an end in themselves. It treats people as commodities, events as trading floors and is characterised by selfish attitudes and behaviour. It is the relational equivalent of the one-night-stand; you get what you want with as little personal cost to yourself as is possible. Perhaps you've been on the receiving end of someone who, in the process of trying to network you, realised that you were not quite what they were looking for and snubbed you in favour of bigger, better prey. Or maybe you've met a person at a networking event who promised the earth but you never heard from them again.

I believe that life's great opportunities and the best new business breakthroughs are far more likely to come from your relationship network than your networking abilities. Turning up in a room full of strangers with the hope of selling yourself or your product is random, impersonal and exceptionally hard work for very little return. It's not smart and it's not sustainable. On the other hand, going through life with a deliberate desire to build new and meaningful relationships, learning how to collect them, keep them and nurture them in the long term, is perhaps the smartest move you'll ever make.

So, back to the invitation to speak at the conference. I explained that I would have to decline the offer to speak at the event. I told them why I was not an advocate of "networking" and explained that I believed in building long term, mutually beneficial relationships based on authenticity and trust.

'Oh,' they said. 'Well, can you speak on that instead?'

I was surprised by their response, but I was even more pleased to still be able to speak at the conference, yet on a subject that I felt comfortable with. Just before I travelled to the event I was a little concerned that I might come off a little negative if I talked about this in terms of anti-networking. Better by far to frame it in the positive, and in one of those lightbulb moments, the inspiration hit me; my field of expertise needed a name, and what better word than *Relationology*?

Who is this book for?

This book is written for people who desire greater life significance and business success. It is written for those who suspect that relationships matter far more than many others suspect. It is written for those who are tired of networking and those who are convinced that there is something better on offer. It is for those who understand the value of integrity, reliability and the importance of other people in our lives. And maybe – just maybe – it is for anyone still hiding behind the sofa.

Perhaps you are a professional adviser such as an accountant, lawyer, management consultant, wealth manager, banker or architect. Or you might work in an advertising agency where you are responsible for new business or client services. This book will be essential for you as you build your client base and then look to develop the lifetime value of your clients.

You could work in a caring profession such as a doctor, dentist, nurse, teacher, police officer, religious leader or charity worker. This book will help you navigate the complex stakeholder relationships you have to manage on a day by day basis. If your purpose involves people then this book is for you.

Whatever you do, the chances are that you don't do it alone. And if that's the case, *Relationology* can help you.

How to use this book?

You can read *Relationology* in a number of ways:

1. Read from beginning to end and ensure you miss nothing! You may want to grab a pen and highlight things that you want to immediately act on.

2. Use the index to identify areas that you are particularly interested in, or to specifically answer a challenge you have in relationships right now. Start by reading that section first.

3. Skim read the entire book and then deep dive into reading secrets that are of specific interest or relevance to you.

Each of the secrets is based on a principle to challenge your thought processes, but also to direct you towards implementing changes in your behaviour and habits.

Who can I talk to?

As you read this book and reflect upon it, please feel free to get in touch. I always like to be enriched by the experiences and knowledge of others:

Twitter – @Relationology

Website – www.relationology.co.uk

Email – mattbird@relationology.co.uk

Thank you for reading!

Matt

Part A: Collect Relationships

Valuing people

Secret 1: You can't be friends with everybody

It was the final round of interviews for an important position within the organisation. The search had been long, the shortlisting rigorous and the interviews themselves thorough in the extreme. But even though the candidates had finally been sent home, there was one final test for them to pass. The executive leading the search stepped out of the conference room and out to the front desk. There he quizzed the receptionists on the behaviour of the candidates as they arrived and left. How did the candidates act as they entered and left the building? Were they friendly? Did they treat the receptionists with warmth and respect, or did they dismiss them out of hand?

The greatest test of our character and integrity is how we treat the people whom we think can do nothing for us.

Is friendliness something that we only switch on when we think it will be strategically advantageous to us? Or is friendliness a fundamental part of who we are? Do we use our smile like our credit card, or is it something irrepressible flowing within us?

This has never been clearer to me than the day I visited 10

Downing Street. After my name had been checked against the list and my passport checked, I was ushered through security and told to walk across the street and through the main entrance, to the iconic black, shiny door. Directed to leave my coat, bag and mobile phone downstairs I finally walked up flights of stairs to the state rooms above. There among the crowd of guests were a handful of government ministers whom I thought it might be interesting to chat to. Plucking up my courage as I walked over, I introduced myself. It only took a fraction of a second for his disinterest in me to be made clear. No smiles, no eye contact, no desire whatsoever to engage in conversation. As soon as was polite, I made my excuses and went to get a drink. The moment I turned around I bumped into another minister. This one could not have been more different. He was smiling, laughing and easily began making conversation. I've never seen either of them since the event – and I probably won't, either – but talking with them was a valuable reminder of just how easy it is to pick up on someone's level of interest in us.

How we treat the receptionist, the stranger at the doorway, the bus driver, the assistant at the supermarket checkout or the waitress in the restaurant tells the world so much about us. Unless we are friendly to everyone our friendliness to a few is not authentic. If we light up our smiles only when we think it might earn us something, we are asking to be mistrusted. We can't be friends with everyone but we can be friendly with everyone.

ACTION: Imagine you watched a film of yourself in action today. How friendly were you with people? What kind of person do you aspire to be? What do you need to change in order to become that person?

Secret 2: Don't open a shop unless you like to smile

I remember making a presentation at an event in a prestigious political venue. The whole occasion was a great success and I left feeling good about how it had gone. The following day one of my close friends asked if I would like a little feedback. At that point I was grateful that as a true friend they'd waited until the following day so that I could enjoy the success a little before learning how I could do better next time. They waxed lyrical about the whole occasion and then said there was one thing that could have made it even better; I could have smiled.

There are few things more important in our communication than our smile. Our smile says a lot about us and what we think of ourselves and the people we are with. A genuine smile says that we are a happy, fulfilled and contented person. It says, I am delighted to be with you, that I recognise you're a great person and I value you. A smile is the universal icebreaker and the best scene setter for a conversation.

A smile is so incredibly powerful, and yet – for some – so often it is seen as an irrelevant optional extra. We all know what happens to those shops and restaurants staffed by stone-faced assistants and waiters; people vote with their feet.

If you've ever spent much time looking at London's police officers you'll probably have noticed that they spend a lot of time talking to each other. It's staggering to think that an organisation which is measured in part on the subjective opinion of public confidence doesn't place a higher premium on having their public-facing workers work a little harder at looking, smiling and chatting with the general public. A little extra friendliness wouldn't cost the tax payer a single pound, but it would transform public confidence.

Not all smiles are equal though, and a fake smile is very easy to spot. It is not enough to simply smile on the outside. A smile must be genuine and come from the inside. Even if you're battling nerves, self-doubt or plain old fashioned fear, think about something happy as you enter a room and allow a smile to break out. Whatever you're about to face will be a whole lot easier as a result.

A smile has nothing to do with beauty, but it has everything to do with connection.

If you want to reach out and start to make better relationships, then this is as basic as it gets; smile. Forget about the Botox and forget about the fear. Remember that when you smile, other people will soften. When you smile, you're open for business.

ACTION: There's nothing complicated about this one; just go out and smile. Over the next twenty-four hours try to view every social interaction as an opportunity to smile. Then do it, watching for the ways in which your encounters play out differently.

Secret 3: Use the magic words

I was overseas, thankful for the hotel air conditioning that kept the humidity at bay. Still, not everything was perfect within the ground floor restaurant, as over the course of an hour I observed two other businessmen in action. They were making constant demands of the staff – fair enough, I suppose – but instead of asking courteously their demands were delivered in barks and half-shouts. There were no smiles, no eye contact and not a single please or thank you. They did not represent themselves at all well.

My three children – Joseph, Matilda and Reuben – have spent their respective nine, six and four years on this planet being drilled in the importance of those "magic words". It's still happening today, with my wife and I reminding them just how vital it is to be polite and say our please and thank yous. Sometimes they remember, sometimes they forget, and when the lesson finally beds in and the drilling can stop, they will have taken a major step in the way they relate to people. My little Relationologists will be making ground.

Whether we're paying for groceries in the supermarket or enjoying a business event, we should practise the habit of being courteous to everyone we have contact with. It demonstrates that we're aware of other people, that we value them for who they are and appreciate what they've done for us.

So why don't we use those key words more? Assuming that we've been drilled a little ourselves when we were children, usually as adults we let them drop because we're too focussed on ourselves, too tired, upset or busy.

Letting the common courtesies slip is a sign that life may well be out of balance.

ACTION: The magic words cost nothing. Go out and use them right now and show that you value people for who they are, not just for what they've done for you. And if you really fancy a challenge, try bringing them into a hard-to-win business encounter. Think about what it feels like to be polite.

Secret 4: Listen with your eyes

We've all been there; mid-way through a conversation with someone when you notice their eyes start to wander from your face to the space over your shoulder. Or, to be more precise, to the rest of the room behind your shoulder. No matter that you were enjoying the chat, those wandering eyes are a clear sign that for the person opposite you, it's all over. There are few things more likely to make us feel like we are not valued by another person. The only thing that's worse than being looked over in this way is being caught in the act yourself, your own wandering eyes betraying your lack of focus.

Not too long ago I asked my elder son what he had learnt at school that day. Normally the question elicits a response along the lines of 'nothing much', but on this particular occasion, he surprised me. 'You should listen twice as much as you speak,' he said. I asked why. 'Because you have been given two ears and only one mouth.' He has a point.

Listening is one of the most important ways to demonstrate that we value the person that we are with.

Rob Parsons, author of *The Heart of Success* tells a powerful story about authentic listening:

'Dad, will you listen to me while I read?'
'I'm listening,' said the dad to his six-year-old daughter, with half an eye on the newspaper headlines.
'Dad, please will you listen to me read?'
'Yes, I am listening,' said the dad, slightly impatiently.

'Silly Daddy, don't you know you have to listen with your eyes as well?'

The truth about listening is that it doesn't just require your ears. It is most powerfully demonstrated when we focus our eyes on the subject as well. This is not easy. It demands that we quieten our mind, turn down the noise of the many pressing matters on our own agenda and be fully – patiently – present. For some of us that is a very hard task indeed.

But as well as being polite, listening with our eyes can also be incredibly revealing. It allows us to take in all the non-verbal communication that is being expressed as well. So many of our nuances and inferences are only expressed by subtle gestures. If you're staring at the exit, you might as well be wearing ear muffs.

When you are with someone who makes you feel like they have no other care in the world other than to listen to you, it is an almost magical experience. Personally, I long to be the kind of person who can listen that well. I'm not there yet, but I'm practising – every single day.

ACTION: Decide to listen as well as you possibly can to the very next person you interact with, even if it means changing your plans.

Secret 5: Make every encounter count

Aren't the best ideas in life so often the simplest? In the film *Pay It Forward*, a class of students are set the challenge of coming up with an idea that will change the world. The main character has an idea that is as simple as they come; pay it forward. He starts a social epidemic simply by doing something kind for three people. They are not allowed to pay him back; instead they are encouraged to pay it forward by each doing something kind for three other people. The idea soon spreads far and wide.

How many examples can you come up with of people being kind to you without wanting anything in return? The more you think, the more you come up with, don't you?

Given that each of us have been on the receiving end of kindnesses of all shapes and sizes, why would we not want to pay it forward? A lift to the airport, a free bit of business advice, an introduction to a valued contact, all of these and more are the things that can make a significant difference in a person's life. They might cost us a lot or very little indeed, but the principle remains the same throughout; being generous makes good business sense.

My own thinking is that if I am going to spend time talking to someone – even if it is for just five minutes – why would I want to send them away empty-handed?

We are resourceful people and it costs us so little to give something of ourselves away to everyone we meet. Think of it as an accelerated living legacy.

And here's one last thought. So many times I have been surprised by the speed with which a good deed returns to me – even though that is not my motive or intention. Let's not waste a single minute – let's make every encounter count.

ACTION: You have seventy-two hours to conceive of – and implement – an act of generosity. Give without expectation of reward. Give because you can!

Building your personal network

Secret 6: Set relationship targets

Golf handicaps, 10k personal bests and the shortest possible time in which you can complete your Friday evening commute; unless we set ourselves a target we're unlikely to maximise our potential.

Put it another way, as anyone who has ever learned to drive knows, we go where we are looking.

But while this works for sport, travel and the family, what if we apply the principle to our relational capital? Instead of simply drifting along, making new relationships only when new ones happen to drift across our path, what if we deliberately set out to add to the number of people with whom we have meaningful contact?

How many new people do you wish to meet this week? How many introductions would you like this month? How many people are you going to ask for a referral before the end of the next quarter?

ACTION: Whenever I confirm attendance at any event I have in mind a number of people I would like to make a meaningful connection with and then add into my network. Why not set a numerical target for the people you want to meet, be introduced or referred to at the next event you attend?

Secret 7: Keep a wish list

Most of us have created a wish list at some point in our lives. Yet, the older we get, the more we seem to find them a little embarrassing. But wish lists don't just belong to the days when we still believed in Father Christmas. In fact, the older we get, the more important I think they become.

Wish lists help to keep us focused. They help to keep in mind the bigger aim and the smaller steps we need to take in order to reach it.

One of my wish lists contains the names of people I really would like to meet. Sometimes people sit on my wish list for a few months while others have been there for years. One of those long-standing names on my list took over a decade before I finally had the opportunity to arrange a meaningful meeting. The wait was worth it – several other meetings followed and subsequently I was invited to become an approved supplier for his business.

At a Relationology event, I challenged the attendees to make a wish list of people they'd like to meet. One man added marketing guru Seth Godin to his list. I smiled as he did so, thinking 'there's a name that's going to be on his list for decades!'

A short while after making the list, the student applied to be part of a small group of people chosen to spend a day with Seth Godin. Despite it being incredibly hard to be selected for this once in a lifetime opportunity, his application was successful, and he got to meet and spend time with the man himself.

For some years my wish lists were always mental ones, however, these lists have become so important to me that I now write them down. And they've got longer and longer. Inspired by my Relationology student I keep on adding names. Who knows where it will all end up?

ACTION: Start your wish list today.

Secret 8: Make a courageous self-introduction

I once read an interview in one of London's newspapers about the incoming CEO of a high street bank. Something about the interview really resonated with me, and so – even though I wasn't entirely sure why I was doing it – I quickly wrote to him, inviting him out for a drink. A few days later, to my surprise and delight I received a reply, accepting my invitation. Even to this day I have no idea why he said yes, but I'm glad he did; a year or so later he was able to host an event for me on the top floor of their corporate head quarters. The evening raised hundreds of thousands of pounds for a community charity.

I like that story, but for every one like it, I have dozens more where the door has been slammed in my face. Even just the other day, having listened to a great interview on the radio I decided to write to the interviewee, explaining that I was convinced that there was a lot of shared interest between us. Would they be interested in an initial meeting to explore the possibility of working together? Their reply was as clear as it was stark; no way.

Self-introductions – these long-shot, out-of-the-blue approaches to people you've never met – require courage.

Will self-introductions all yield positive replies? Of course not. In my experience the positives are in the absolute minority, yet that does not stop me from continuing to reach out to people, introduce myself and suggest a meeting.

Of course, the times when a courageous self-introduction

works and the person says yes to meeting makes all those rejections bearable. Reach out often enough, and it won't be long before you'll find yourself on a markedly different path to the one you were on before.

ACTION: Who could you courageously introduce yourself to today?

Secret 9: Be the recipient of trust transfer

The clock was ticking. I was weeks away from hosting a national event for various CEOs of social enterprises and there was a senior government official who I wanted to secure as the keynote speaker. There was just one problem; I had never met the official and had no obvious connection to them. Intuition told me that this was the sort of occasion where the courageous self-introduction was not the required approach.

So I asked around, found a common acquaintance and asked if they would make an introduction. A kind introduction was made, followed up by a carefully worded letter, which led to a meeting and finally acceptance to speak at the event. Bingo!

Getting yourself introduced by a mutual acquaintance is one of the ways of dramatically increasing the odds of a positive response in situations like this.

When your initial meeting is going to be used to pitch an idea or opportunity, then it is vital that you have established a level of trust between you. A mutual acquaintance can help with this, transferring trust in the process. You are benefitting from the credibility the introducer has built up over the years with the person they are introducing you to.

ACTION: Who would you like to meet? Who do you need to meet? What mutual acquaintances do you share? When and how are you going to ask if they would make an introduction? Make a list – as well as a plan.

Secret 10: Identify multi-relaters

Not everybody's address book is the same size. Some have a natural tendency towards a smaller circle of those they connect with, while others seem to know absolutely everyone and have a talent for making friends wherever they go.

Marcus Buckingham of the Gallup Organisation describes talent as what we cannot help but do. Of the thirty-four talents that Gallup identify, "WOO" (Winning Others Over) is one of the most valuable to the student of Relationology.

If we have this talent, strangers aren't intimidating – in fact, they're fascinating people that we want to talk to and get to know.

But what if we don't have "woo"? The answer's simple. In choosing relationships, make sure you include some of these multi-relaters, the very ones with the super-sized list of contacts. Multi-relaters can help us meet hordes of new people, and therefore accelerate the growth of our personal network, saving us years in the process.

How to spot them? The chances are that they'll find you, but if you want to head out and track some down today, there are a range of professions that tend to attract a high percentage of multi-relaters:

Restaurateurs
Headhunters
Lobbyists
Fundraisers

Public relations
Politicians
Journalists
Teachers
Pastors

ACTION: If making masses of new connections is not your scene, find – or let yourself be found by – a multi-relater and see where their influence takes you. And if you happen to have plenty of WOO and a large contact list, try reaching out to someone who's not like you today. What can you learn from each other?

Secret 11: Join a professional network

Recently I joined a professional network called the Professional Speakers Association. It exists to help public speakers improve both their delivery and their network, and I was a little unsure of what to expect when I attended my first event. I immediately met two other speakers in my field of expertise who have become friends and are challenging me to raise my game. There was a professional photographer offering head shots at a discounted price which now appear on my social media profiles. During the day I heard some incredible speakers and was profoundly challenged to work at my personal excellence. All in all it was a brilliant day and represented great value. I'll certainly be going again.

There is a wide variety of professional networks out there, and the chances are that you could join any number of them, from trade bodies and professional development organisations to alumni and networking groups.

And just as there are multiple options, there are various reasons for joining a professional network; you are highly likely to meet a handful of people that you hit it off with and who you can then add to your personal network.

By joining a network that is recognised within your industry or sector, your personal brand will benefit – particularly if you have an opportunity to sit on a working group, speak at an event or contribute to a publication.

Finally, when you start to mix with others who work in your

field, you will inevitably start to benchmark yourself against them – and when you're mixing with the best in the business, you're bound to see yourself improve.

ACTION: Ask around and discover what professional networks your colleagues and clients are members of and consider which would be most beneficial for you. Check out the membership benefits, criteria and fees and join up. Alternatively you may already be a member of a professional network and you just need to become an active participant. What are you waiting for?

Flourishing in a crowded room

Secret 12: Join the energy in the room

Crowded rooms can be daunting places, and walking through the doors on our own can cause even the most confident person to pause and wonder how best they can get through the initial pain barrier of deciding where – and how – to start.

Most of us will scan the faces in search of someone we know. If it's a good friend, then so much the better, but – depending on your level of anxiety – often almost anyone will do. It's not a bad idea on its own, but it's hardly going to help you meet anyone new, is it? The chances are that you'll simply cling to each other for far too long, missing out on who knows how many brilliant new conversations and connections.

But what if you adopted a different approach? Admittedly, it requires a good deal more courage than simply cosying up to your friends, but the potential payback is significant. In the time it takes you to walk to the bar and pick up a drink, or head for a waiter with a tray, try scanning the room.

You're on the lookout for the group of people who are the most animated and making the most noise. Once you have your drink in hand, it is to these people that you then go and introduce yourself.

ACTION: Some of you love the idea, while others are recoiling in horror. Either way, the next time you pass through the doors alone, remember to search for the hub of the room's relational energy and ask yourself; wouldn't you rather be a part of what's going on over there?

Secret 13: Practise the graceful entrance

Someone, somewhere (it was me, on the previous page) once told you to search out the chattiest, most animated group whenever you enter a room on your own. So, having decided to put the advice into practice at the next social event you attend solo, you walk over to the cluster of laughing people, shuffle yourself into their circle and wait for someone to acknowledge you. And then you wait a bit longer. And eventually, feeling utterly humiliated and ignored, you back away from the group and retreat to the bar.

The truth is that spotting the energy in a room and deciding to join it are vital steps, but they're not the whole journey; you have to have something to say when you get there.

There are many ways to make a graceful entrance to a group in the midst of conversation. Sometimes simply walking up and standing in the circle actually is enough – but only if the group itself is observant, generous and kind. At most other times it is necessary to insert yourself into the conversation. But how? Do we just walk up and say "Hello"? Again, this can work, but there's a chance that the group will not easily allow its flow to be stopped like this – as I've learned from bitter experience.

And so we must learn something better – the graceful entrance. I can't ever remember it failing, although it does require bundles of relational confidence. Approach the group and stand next to the person who is speaking, as you do so gently touch their arm.

The physical contact is like an electric shock – the person who was speaking stops and looks to you, and in that moment you begin a conversation.

Admittedly, this is not an approach for the fainthearted, and you need to be ready to lead the conversation, but trust me – it really works.

ACTION: Try to make a graceful entrance at the next social event you attend. And if you're not quite ready for that, make a point of watching how others do it. What else can you learn from them?

Secret 14: Use names immediately

Recently, I committed a terrible faux pas. I was thinking about one person while talking to another and got their names muddled up. Instead of saying Nathan I called him Simon and he just stood there, staring at me, wincing slightly. Fortunately, it was one of my nine-year-old son's friends, and the two of them thought it was all a bit of a joke and decided to spend the rest of the afternoon mixing up everybody's name.

Remembering people's names is a very real challenge, especially when we're meeting lots of people for the first time and we are aware of the consequences of getting it wrong. So what do we do?

Firstly, we need to worry less about the fact that we might forget, and concentrate on ways that will help us to remember. Using someone's name to address them directly makes a profoundly positive impact on not just our memory, but also on the person themselves.

People love to hear their name used, especially when in a group of people.

There are a number of ways to remember. I like to use a name about three times within the first three minutes of a conversation, and it rarely sounds as forced as some might fear. If the name is at all unusual then so much the better; asking how it is spelt provides a further opportunity to picture the name and learn it.

If we do forget an individual's name during the first conversation there are ways to remedy this. We can either simply say, 'I'm so sorry, please remind me of your name,' or if that's too awkward, simply ask them for their business card. Simple!

ACTION: Make a list of the people whose names you seem to have trouble remembering. Write them down and learn them.

Secret 15: Be completely present

Now and again my wife will ask me, 'Where are you?' I look at her blankly and then realise what she means. I may be physically present with her and the kids, but my mind has drifted off elsewhere.

It happens when we are away from the home as well. The length of our to-do list, the imminence of the looming deadline, the following day's meeting that we really do need to prepare for – all these things that remove us from the present and distract us. And when our attention wanders, others will notice.

The key to avoiding this is to become completely present, to engage with your eyes, mind and whole being.

Yet it is an art that cannot be learned overnight. Instead, it can only be developed and perfected through patience and practice. When you find yourself tempted to think about something other than the person in front of you, stop and notice what your senses are telling you about the moment and place you are in. It doesn't mean ignoring the pressures that are on us, but it does mean valuing the person you're facing and putting those distractions on hold, if only for the duration of your conversation.

So let's dig deep. Let's exercise the self-management muscles that will enable us to be completely present with the people we are with, whoever they are. Isn't it how we'd like others to treat us?

ACTION: The next time you find yourself struggling to be in the moment, turn off your phone, close the laptop and breathe. Be fully present and notice what's unique about the moment.

Secret 16: Translate cultural codes

A friend of mine had just moved to London. He'd been invited to attend a dinner party "at 7.30pm for 8pm". Not wanting to be rude, he arrived promptly at 7.30pm and was surprised that his hosts were still dressing for dinner.

He was not the first of my friends to have found the cultural codes of the English rather confusing. So many times we say one thing but mean something completely different. We talk about the weather, but not because we want to have a detailed discussion of evidence-based meteorology, but simply because we want to allow the conversation to warm up slowly. We ask someone how they are, but without wishing to endure a detailed medical history or run down a list of current ailments or issues.

We simply are indicating that we would like to talk to them and invite them to say something interesting about themselves.

And then there are the words "it's been nice talking to you". In any other cultural context this would be an invitation to continue the pleasant conversation, but not for us British. It means that the conversation is now over and it's high time I was allowed to move on and talk to somebody else.

ACTION: In these days when business in the UK is increasingly international, there is no longer one set of cultural codes in play. Keep an eye out for the different nuances and messages that people are communicating. Who will you meet in the next week that has a different set of cultural assumptions to you?

Secret 17: Never go to the party empty-handed

A friend and I both attended an event hosted by the Prime Minister. On a rare break from meeting new people (see Secret 12), we stood and chatted. He told me that he had been thinking about what he would say to our host if he had the opportunity. As it happened, that's exactly what occurred, when the Prime Minister walked through the room chatting to guests, he bumped into my friend.

Never go to the party empty-handed. I'm not talking about chocolates, flowers or wine. I'm talking about words.

Here are four things I try to take to any and every meeting, reception, event, party or conference:

Gift 1: An awareness of what's in the news

It doesn't take long to check out the news on your phone before arriving at an event. It provides you with an opportunity to lead in conversation by asking, 'Have you heard the news about …?' or if you are asked that question then you are able to give your views on the matter.

Gift 2: Answer to 'How are you?'

As I mentioned earlier, we all need to be ready to translate the question 'How are you?' It's not a question about your health and wellbeing but an invitation to say something interesting about yourself. What personal story have you got up your sleeve to offer as a response?

Gift 3: Elevator Pitch

It's only a matter of time before somebody asks you 'What do you do?' Imagine you are in an elevator and at floor three someone enters the lift and in conversation they ask you, 'What do you do?' You are exiting the lift at floor twelve so you know you have nine floors, or roughly sixty seconds to communicate. Being able to answer in a way that both identifies your business and distinguishes it from others is important. And while it might sound like a short elevator ride, sixty seconds can be a long time to talk about yourself in an interesting, engaging way.

Gift 4: VIP Conversation

When you go to an event or conference, expect to meet the host or keynote speaker. In fact I'd suggest that you make it your business to go and introduce yourself to them. Prior to the event think about what you will say to them in order to create a good impression and begin to build rapport with them.

ACTION: Make sure you're ready to talk about who you are and what you do so that people remember you, understand what you're passionate about and start to share with you their own stories and hopes.

Secret 18: Compliment people

'David has told me so much about you. It is a delight to meet you.'

As compliments go, this one that I received at the start of a dinner party still ranks as one of my all-time highs. Hearing someone pay you a genuine compliment can make for one of those moments in life when a warm glow shoots through your whole being.

In general, people do not think of themselves as highly as they should.

In the vast majority of cases, paying someone a compliment does not risk feeding an over-developed sense of self-importance. Most of the time, a compliment is a welcome and much-needed gift of human interaction and affirmation.

A core requirement of making a compliment is that it be genuine. Compliments have an uncanny transparency about them, so whatever we say it had better be for real. There is no need to lay it on too thick or expand beyond a simple sentence, but it needs to be authentic.

ACTION: How often do you compliment people? Will you go out of your way today to make other people feel good about themselves? Can you receive them as well as hand them out?

Secret 19: Make the most of business cards

At some point in our working lives, most of us have had a block of unused business cards sat in a drawer, going absolutely nowhere. Perhaps we keep on forgetting to put them into our pocket, or perhaps the whole notion of handing out the tiny slips of card leaves us cringing with embarrassment.

We've all got cards that have been given to us by people we really can't quite remember. Their cards clog up our bags and hide in the deepest pockets of last year's winter coat. In these days of social media, why do people bother with business cards at all anyway?

I want to reclaim the business card as an effective tool of social engagement.

To do that, I believe that we need to relearn how to use them. These four simple techniques will show you how.

Technique 1: When do you give a business card? *Straight away.*

In my experience, one of the best moments to pass a business card to someone that I have just met is when they enquire, 'What is it you do?' In that moment I simultaneously reach for a business card from my pocket and begin to explain that I have created a new social science, Relationology. Alternatively, I wait until the end of the conversation to perform the exchange, however there is always the risk that the conversation will be interrupted and the opportunity will be lost.

Technique 2: Should you expect to receive one in return? *Absolutely.*

Of all the many thousands of business cards that I have given out over the years, only a very small percentage of people have ever contacted me as a result. So the only way to guarantee being able to be in contact with a person having met them once, is if you have their contact details as well. Sometimes people run out of business cards, so rather than hand yours over and expect them to email you their details (which they may forget to do anyway), I reach for a jotter that I keep in my jacket pocket and invite them to scribble down their mobile and email (I find people automatically start with their name).

Technique 3: What do you do with the business card? *Throw it away.*

As soon as is reasonably possible – often for me that means the time when I am travelling between meetings – I store the name, business, role, email and mobile (for most of us the postal addresses and fax number are completely irrelevant, so save your time). Either I'll do this by entering the data into my phone or by photographing the card and emailing it to my office. I might add a note of who introduced me to the person, or the event that we met at, so if I can't remember the person's name I can always do a search on my database and find them another way. Once that's done, it goes in the bin.

Technique 4: What do you do next? *Follow through*.

Whenever I meet someone that I would genuinely like to keep in contact with, I always, always, always drop them a note afterwards. This may be as simple as an email with a warm greeting, followed by a casual reminder of where we met, a very brief reference to what we discussed and a line such as, "It would be great to keep in contact from time to time". This has the benefit of reinforcing my name and marking me out from most other people they met at that event who will not follow through.

ACTION: Get out that dusty box of business cards today and make them work for you. How quickly can you give away fifty of them?

Secret 20: Practice the graceful exit

All good things come to an end, and so having enjoyed a really great conversation with a complete stranger at a drinks party or business event, you become aware of the need to move on. That's when the inevitable question arises; how do you get out of a conversation well? It's a challenge that makes entering a conversation look positively easy.

If you are about to leave the party or event, then it's rather easy to explain you now have to make a move. But what if you're staying yet want to move on to another conversation? There are lots of approaches that I use, and I'm sure you've probably got a few ideas tucked up your sleeves also – in which case, why not email me (mattbird@relationology.co.uk) and we'll trade a few?

Here, though, are my old faithful techniques for a graceful exit:

A good line is to ask, 'Would you like another drink?' If the answer is no then you are free to excuse yourself, nip off to the bar and meet someone else. If the answer is yes then I suggest you say, 'Shall we both go to the bar?' during which time you are both sure to get talking to other people. Don't offer to go and fetch the drinks though, otherwise you could end up back at square one.

An alternative is to say, 'I don't want to keep you to myself, you probably want to chat to some other people.' Or perhaps use the more subtle option – as long as they can translate the cultural code – 'It's been great talking to you', or even, 'I've really enjoyed speaking to you, let's go and chat to some other people.'

One of my favourite graceful exits – and this is a real trade secret – is to say, 'There is someone I'd like you to meet, can I introduce you?'

No one ever says no. Both parties are delighted because they have been introduced as someone the other person should meet. In addition, having made the initial introduction you can naturally slip away to talk to someone else.

ACTION: Try the graceful exit whenever you're next at an event or function. How does it feel? What do you notice about how well it works?

Turning a stranger into a friend

Secret 21: Small talk is the prelude to big talk

How good are you at making small talk in a room full of strangers? Some of us have personalities that find the thought of this quite exhausting. Others of us find the idea electrifying. Whatever our personality, the ability to make small talk can in large part be determined by our mood. In the right frame of mind, we can flourish. In the wrong state, we can bomb.

First of all, let's get to basics; why even bother with small talk? Aren't all those questions – How are you? Where are you from? What do you do? When do you think the weather will turn? – rather trivial and inconsequential?

I don't think they are. In fact, I think they're some of the most important conversations we can ever have. Why? Because by breaking the ice and enabling another person to feel relaxed, small talk allows someone to show themselves at their best and begin to trust us. My own experience is that once the ice is broken and I have established a natural rapport with others, we can move on to more consequential topics. I have lost count of the number of business opportunities that have resulted from simple conversations that started like this.

So how do we get ourselves in the right mood for small talk?

In the same way that music can relax us ready for a

night in, or energise us for a night out, the "music" we play in our mind before we head into a crowded room can prepare us for making small talk.

Remember those moments when you have been your very best at small talk. Failing that, picture yourself flourishing in a crowded room. And if you're really struggling, practise. Try striking up conversation with a taxi driver, waiter or policeman. In time it will become easier and easier, eventually bringing you to the point where you have the skill of being able to talk to anyone.

Remember that like even the mightiest trees, deep relationships always start from a shallow beginning. So delight in small talk, don't despise it.

ACTION: Imagine you are preparing to go to a business event where you are going to meet lots of new people. What are you hoping will be your three best conversation starters?

Secret 22: Authentic listening

Hands, eyes, shoulders, tone of voice and even the way we arrange our feet – over 80% of communication is non verbal. If we want to be an authentic listener, we must learn to take notice of the full range of communication tools that are being used in front of us.

Listening in this way is a powerful tool. It allows you to feed back what you hear to the speaker, to re-state or paraphrase in your own words what you have heard in order to confirm the mutual understanding in each party. I use it all the time, with CEOs and my three little children; it matters to me that they know I'm listening to them.

Authentic listening is actually a gift rather than a learnt technique.

To really listen to someone you have to be prepared to suspend your agenda, to pause the urge to line up and deliver your next comment as soon as possible. Authentic listeners are comfortable with a moments silence and are prepared to have their minds changed as a result of the conversation. Authentic listeners hear and understand.

In a society that is full of background noise and flickering distractions, authentic listening is a much needed art in our society. Try it and I am sure that, like me, you will find that people thrive when they feel as though they have someone who is genuinely listening to them.

ACTION: Who are the people you are seeing this week who you could make the gift of "authentic listening" to?

Secret 23: It is more important to be interested

On occasion, people have confessed to me that they don't think they're a very interesting person. While I might disagree with them, it is hard to convince someone in a simple, single conversation that they are wrong about this. What's more, I'm not all that sure that being interesting should be the goal that every one of us is aiming for. Far more important is that we find other people interesting.

Dale Carnegie, when asked about how to make people love us, wrote about how important it is that we become genuinely interested in other people. Stephen Covey, author of *The Seven Habits of Highly Effective People*, explains that we need to understand others before asking them to understand us. The motivational speaker Zig Ziglar says that people don't care about how much we know until they know how much we care. There is a big theme here, and at the heart of it is the part that being interested in people plays in building a rapport with them.

To be genuinely interested requires real selflessness and a lowering of our self-orientation.

Being interested means that we need to be ready and willing to pause the discussion about ourselves or our own special "thing". It means being willing to give all the air time to the person we are with. However, what goes around comes around because on most occasions the more we find out about the other person, the more they will want to find out about us.

Showing interest isn't just about asking the right questions. It's also about smiling, laughing and being energetic in the way we engage. It's no good saying, 'So, tell me what you're excited about at the moment,' if our face and posture indicate that we couldn't care less what the answer is.

Developing the capacity to be more interested in other people is a breakthrough skill in Relationology. It marks the difference between a good leader and a great leader.

ACTION: Who are the people who show the greatest interest in you? How do they do it and what can you learn from them?

Secret 24: Curiosity only killed the cat

Imagine yourself at a business dinner or family wedding, sitting next to a stranger. They are infinitely curious about you. They ask about your life, your work, your interests, what makes you tick, what ticks you off, your hopes and aspirations and your worries and fears. Then turn to the person on the other side of you and experience their near-total indifference to you and everything about you. Every conversational morsel that you offer up is treated with the same bored disinterest.

Which side would you rather talk to?

Curiosity may have killed the cat, but it certainly makes for great conversation.

Curiosity is playful and inquisitive, and it invites the person to open up and tell us more. All that it requires is the use of open questions – the sort that begin with what, why, where, when and how. Curiosity avoids closed questions where a simple "yes" or "no" would suffice. The curious questioner is open and honest, often starting out with phrases like 'I'm curious how…' or 'Tell me more about…'

I once had the privilege of seeing an absolute master in action. The fact that they were a member of the royal family was impressive enough to get my attention, but what blew me away was the way that they moved around the room, engaging in small talk, listening, showing interest, asking questions and making comments themselves. It changed the atmosphere and left people inspired and energised.

ACTION: What can you change about your language to help you to become more curious?

Secret 25: Put yourself at risk

Being professional is about looking, speaking, playing and thinking the part. However, the cut-throat world of the 1980s are long gone, and – thankfully – today we allow ourselves to show our more vulnerable side.

Yet vulnerability isn't just about being open with our peers or superiors. Apologising or admitting failure to a junior colleague – if done in the correct way – can garner respect and be a great example of leadership. In the 1992 US presidential campaign, several comments were made about Clinton's personal flaws. Instead of putting out a message of denial, Clinton's advisors told him to play on them and emphasise the importance of being human and vulnerable. This became known as the Manhattan Project. Clinton won the campaign and became America's forty-second president.

Vulnerability can be as simple as ensuring that we express our humanity by talking (appropriately) about our private lives with people and avoiding projecting ourselves as superhuman. Vulnerability can be talking about how we feel about things, whether personal or professional. It can even be making a self-disclosure about our inner world. The key to making vulnerability an asset rather than a liability is understanding what makes for an appropriate level of self-disclosure based on the stage of the relationship and the context of the conversation.

If that all sounds too much for you, then bear in mind that vulnerability can also be expressed when we say that we don't know the answer to a question or a query, or whenever we ask for help or admit failure.

One of the city firms that I work with teaches its team "business intimacy". This is about building a stronger relationship with trusted clients by bringing your whole self to work. As writer Rob Parsons once said, 'If you share your achievements you can win a contact, but if you share your fears you can make a friend.'

Being vulnerable and putting yourself at risk says to the other person that you trust them and that you want to know them at a deeper, more meaningful level.

Surely this is where we want to be in our relationships? How are you going to get there?

ACTION: Discuss with someone you are close to the degree to which you are vulnerable in your relationship – both with them and others. In what ways could you be more open and vulnerable?

Securing an initial meeting

Secret 26: Win over the gatekeeper

If there's one person you will ever need to win over in order to secure an initial meeting, it is the personal assistant. The PA is the formally appointed gatekeeper who holds the power to bump us off the list of possible contacts. So how do you win over the gatekeeper? Experience has taught me two keys:

Respect their role

Just like you and me, PAs have a job to do so we need to respect it. They are likely to have tried and tested processes and systems for everything they do. So if you want to win them over, respect their way of working and go with their flow.

Respect them

The PA's role is very functional, and so on the whole they enjoy the opportunity for non-functional conversations. I have found that they become more chatty once they have spoken to me two or three times. In part, they need to know you respect what they do and they need time to establish you're not some chancer who is stalking their boss. Sometimes PAs do not want to engage in chit chat – not much discernment is required for this, as they tend to make themselves very clear when this is the case, but make sure you spot it.

Once the PA is on side, you should find securing your initial meeting and any subsequent meetings is a whole lot easier.

ACTION: Take a pad of paper and write down the names of your ten most valuable clients. Then make a note of their PAs' names and anything you know about them.

Secret 27: Smile on the telephone

I remember making a phone call from home. I was slouching in a chair, with my feet up on the desk generally feeling a bit weary. After five minutes the person on the other end asked, 'Are you ok? You don't sound your normal self.' It was in that moment that I realised just how important the non-verbal aspects of communication are, even when the other person couldn't see me. Our body posture and facial posture affect our tone of voice.

Even when we are on the phone, our non-verbal communication matters. So when you make any telephone call – but especially the one that you hope will secure an initial meeting – think about what people will hear in your voice. What is your body posture? What is your facial expression? What is your frame of mind?

Now, I always try to smile while I'm on the phone.

Even though people can't see my smile, they can hear it. I also tend to walk around my office. Even though people can't see the alertness and energy in my body posture, they can hear it in my voice.

ACTION: Recollect one of your most effective business calls. What was your frame of mind and what was your body posture? If you were to develop three new telephone habits what would they be?

Secret 28: Acknowledge busyness

Put yourself in the shoes of the person you are trying to meet: they have a list of roles and responsibilities, both personal and professional. At times this busyness is overwhelming. Then they hear from someone (you) who they met briefly at a meeting, reception or dinner who wants to meet again. They are uncertain that they have capacity for anything else in their life so it's easier to simply not reply, decline or defer your suggestion.

Busyness comes to us all. We don't often seek it out, but before we know it we can find ourselves flat out busy. When I'm busy I sometimes find myself being curt in my responses to people and not treating them with the respect and value I desire. When I'm busy I sometimes become less creative and less innovative because I have no time and space to think.

Our aim should be driving us towards being purposeful rather than busy, which is why I build dimensions into my routine to help mitigate against busyness, yet busyness continues to try and dominate my life.

When you are working to secure an initial meeting, acknowledge that you recognise they are a busy person and that their time is valuable. This understanding and empathy about their situation helps, and it also makes the person think that they're probably not too busy and can make space to meet you.

ACTION: Take a look at your diary and ask yourself whether you're simply busy or purposeful. What changes do you need to make in order to encourage more of the latter and less of the former?

Secret 29: Set expectations

There are occasions when most of us have been at the receiving end of a meeting that had an agenda we were not expecting. On occasions, I've been hosted for one-to-one meetings or receptions which, once they were under way, I realised were about raising funds for a business or a charity when I was given the impression they were about something else. At other times I've met up with someone for what I thought was an informal catch up, only to be sprung with a hardcore pitch for work. In these moments we can feel hoodwinked into something we were not expecting.

When trying to secure an initial meeting, it is often a prerequisite, if not a simple courtesy, to communicate the reasons for the meeting. Setting expectations for meetings can prevent people from feeling manipulated. There are three general expectations you can set for a meeting:

Agenda

Some initial meetings have a clear agenda. If you have built enough rapport during the initial informal conversation, simply saying, 'I would like to meet to discuss an opportunity,' is sufficient to set expectations. If you are unknown to the person you are requesting a meeting with, you will most often need to be more specific.

Open Agenda

Some initial meetings have an open agenda where

there is no set plan or purpose. There is an openness to getting to know one another, and the possibility of doing something together. In this scenario saying something along the lines of 'I would like to meet you and to get to know you and see what happens,' is enough to set expectations.

No Agenda

Meetings with no agenda are generally the exclusive preserve of a long-standing friendship, which may exist in both our personal and our professional worlds. It is possible that an initial meeting may have no agenda, however it is more likely to have an open agenda.

Intuition, and common sense, are required in order to know which way to play an initial meeting.

Not enough agenda and some people may think you are wasting their time, too much agenda and some people make think you are pushy. Agility is required.

ACTION: Reflect on the last three meetings you have had with prospective clients – you may have to flick back through your diary. In each case was there too much or too little agenda? What are you going to change about the next meeting with a prospective client?

Secret 30: Ask for wisdom

What would it take for you to accept a request for an initial meeting with someone you have never met? There are many factors that influence me to take such a meeting, so I try and apply these factors when I'm trying to secure a meeting with someone whom I have never met.

One of the factors that influences me is humility. There is nothing so unappealing in someone than the sense that they think they know it all. Contrastingly, there is nothing so winsome as someone who has a life-long learning posture.

When I request an initial meeting with someone, it is most often because there is something that I think I can learn from them.

So my agenda is often about asking for their advice about a particular subject or issue. There is nothing quite as flattering as being asked for your wisdom about a specific matter.

ACTION: What problems are you currently trying to navigate through? Who do you admire and respect? Find and ask for advice from the people you trust and respect.

Secret 31: Assume people will forget you are meeting

I was out of town preparing to speak at an event when my mobile phone pinged. The message left me horrified:

"Arrived at your club, sat in the foyer."

It reminded me of the time I arrived in someone's office only to discover that the person I thought I was meeting with was far, far away on holiday.

Save yourself heaps of time and lots of embarrassment and assume that each appointment that you have in your diary has accidentally fallen out of the diary of those you are meeting. As a matter of routine my meetings are confirmed in three ways:

> Immediate
>
> Whenever an appointment is made in my diary, my PA or I write an email immediately confirming the date, time, place and agenda of the meeting.
>
> Week prior
>
> Up to a week prior to the meeting we write again to "confirm arrangements".
>
> On the day
>
> On the day of the appointment I will text the person I am meeting to say that I'm looking forward to

seeing them, and then adding the details of the time and place.

From time to time, one of these three confirmations will receive a reply along the lines of, "Thank you so much for the note, it had slipped out of my diary but I'm pleased that it is now confirmed."

Occasionally the response is, "I'm so sorry there has been a miscommunication, would you mind if we reschedule?" Do I mind? Of course I don't. By checking first, we've both saved a whole lot of time and embarrassment.

ACTION: Remember a time when you or someone you are meeting has messed up on the arrangements to meet. What would it have taken to avoid the error?

Secret 32: Reach out again

Many years ago, I had the good fortune to be introduced to a very senior public figure. The only reason I got through the door was because of my introducer and the good old "trust transfer" effect (see Secret 9). However, in the run up to the meeting I started to believe that this event might well end up being one of those glorious, but one-off, encounters.

In advance of the meeting, I mentioned my concerns to a friend and he advised me that one of the most important questions I needed to ask myself was how was I going to get in the room with the person again. So in preparation for the meeting, I came up with an idea about how to reach out to him to ensure that we met again. It worked, and since we have developed a long-standing relationship.

Once you have secured your initial meeting, ask yourself how are you going to reach out in order to see that person again. Perhaps you have a business opportunity that could be explored, a charitable cause that could benefit from their support or simply you know a restaurant they would really enjoy. The list of possibilities is as long as your creativity.

Getting beyond the first meeting is not easy with people in senior positions, but it is by no means impossible.

These days I seem to get it mostly right, however, there are still occasions when I fail miserably.

ACTION: How many of your first time meetings with a prospective client have gone no further? What could you change about your approach to improve your strike rate?

Overcoming self-doubt

Secret 33: There is no such thing as can't

As I write this book I'm wrestling with my demons. There are times when I find the process of writing particularly hard work, and I hear myself start to claim that "I can't write". Before I know it I start reminding myself that I was in remedial English classes for a time at school, and I remind myself of the verdict I laid on myself all those years ago; that I'm stupid. Everything begins to spiral. No wonder I can't write in a mood like this.

You would be less than human if you never wrestled with self-doubt. In those moments your self-confidence and self-motivation can be diluted and diminished. But none of us need to stay in such a miserable place. The remedy begins with being honest with yourself and asking what are the situations that are currently causing you to feel twinges of self-doubt? It may be as simple as:

A phone call you need to make.
A face to face conversation you need to have.
A person you need to go and see.
A presentation you need to start preparing for.
A new opportunity you want to reach out for.

The clichés abound when it comes to the topic of our battles with self-doubt in the struggle for success; success is 90% perspiration and only 10% inspiration. Success is not achieved by spectators but by those people who try and try and try again. Winners never quit and quitters never win.

There is no such thing as can't.

The reason why they're clichés is because they're true. The wisdom is well worn and familiar to so many of us. We dismiss these words at our peril.

ACTION: Consider what you would really like to do but you have not yet done because you've believed you can't. What self-limiting belief are you going to change?

Secret 34: Super humans are humans too

When we spend time meeting people, it is inevitable that we will start to compare ourselves to others. And when we start comparing ourselves with others, it is equally inevitable that – sooner or later – we will find ourselves dealing with feelings of inadequacy, inferiority and even intimidation.

The more successful the person is, the greater the temptation to doubt our own abilities. It is in those moments when we are feeling insecure that we need to remind ourselves that the wealthy, powerful or beautiful person we look up to is every bit as human as we are. Wealthy people worry whether or not they have enough money to never need to work again. Powerful people worry about who might betray them and put them in tomorrow's papers. Beautiful people worry about losing their looks. We all worry. We are all human.

Learning to be relaxed and confident around people who have achieved significant success can be hugely advantageous. Just by being with them you can absorb their winning mindset and abundance thinking.

Successful people find themselves surrounded by people who want something from them, so it's hardly surprising that one of the challenges they face is knowing who they can trust.

They are often in a position where they have everything to lose and others have everything to gain. One of the antidotes to this problem is to focus on what you can give to enrich the life of another rather than on how you can benefit as a result.

In fact, engaging with people because you want to enrich their lives rather than benefit from them is a great model to follow – regardless of the person's standing.

ACTION: Who do you know who is supremely resourceful? Over the next month take time to do something for them that no-one else would think to do.

Secret 35: Replay your success

Just recently, I was completing an application form and updating my CV for a non-executive director role. As I was doing so, I began to think, 'I hope they don't call me for interview as the panel would obviously know much more about everything than me.'

I wouldn't be at all surprised if you had faced a situation recently where you felt intimidated or out of your depth. It might have been a telephone call, a pitch for a piece of work or an application for a new role, but whatever the situation, the end result was the same; you were left facing those old feelings of self-doubt.

My third secret for overcoming these struggles is to replay success. When you are tempted to give in to insecurity, replay your success:

Recall

Recall a time in your life when you have known success. What have you done that you are most proud of? When have you operated at your best? What times of success can you recall?

Remind

Remind yourself of the thoughts and feelings you experienced at that time. Did you feel excited, delighted, filled with self-belief and renewed confidence? What thoughts and feelings can you remind yourself of?

Replay

Replay the picture of what you did, what the results were and especially the thoughts and feelings you experienced at the time. If you can achieve something once you can undoubtedly do it again. This is the magic moment, so replay it and enjoy it.

Why not get ahead of the game and start thinking now about a handful of times when you enjoyed real success.

Start working on a selection of memories to bring to mind at the point when you need them most.

ACTION: Recall a time when you knew great success. Remind yourself of the thoughts and feelings you experienced and replay the whole scene in your mind.

Secret 36: Play in your sweet spot

My third secret for overcoming feelings of self-doubt is to play in your sweet spot by focusing on your strengths. Of course, there are times and places to extend yourself, however the moment when you are wrestling with self-doubt may not be the best time. At these times it is wise to return to the muscle memory of what you know best.

In the world of sport the sweet spot is that special place on the racket or bat that produces the optimum response. It's the perfect balance of tool and technique, and the concept translates to life and relationships as well. You might find that you're operating in your own personal sweet spot whenever you are talking about a subject matter with which you are very familiar, using a skill that you have practiced endless times or mixing with people in a social setting where you feel at ease and confident. Maybe it's going for a run, digging in the garden, planning some grand new business scheme or teaching your kids how to build the biggest Lego model they've ever seen (see Secret 37).

Your sweet spot is the place where you are your most authentic self.

ACTION: The next time you feel overwhelmed and worried that you're not matching up, carve out some time to do the thing that reminds you of what it feels like to really enjoy yourself. Get in your sweet spot and you'll gain a new perspective on the situation that previously troubled you.

Secret 37: Imagine them playing Lego

Years ago I remember feeling extremely intimidated by a senior city executive. I'm not sure precisely what it was that used to intimidate me most about him – perhaps it was the importance of his job, the penthouse office, the mansion-like holiday home, the helicopter or the seeming invincibility of his confidence. Whatever it was, I'd feel nervous and insecure whenever I was around him.

Then something changed. The turning point, for which I will always be grateful, was visiting him in his home. I saw a different side of him; softer, warmer, more human and approachable. He'd call out his children's names – always adding the word "bear" onto the end – and I watched him get down on the floor, surrounded by a small mountain of Lego, and play with his children, laughing with them and encouraging them all the time. My perception of him was transformed.

As sure as the sun will rise in the morning and set again in the evening, there are people who you feel intimidated by.

Regardless of whether your feelings are entirely logical or ridiculously random, such insecurities may well drive you to inaction, leaving you stalled and stuck.

Next time those feelings are triggered, imagine the person on the floor with their children or grandchildren, playing Lego or doing something else as equally mundane and ordinary. See them happy, relaxed, unguarded and free. It's a simple visualisation technique, but it's extremely powerful and will transform how you feel amongst people that threaten to intimidate you.

Thinking about Lego-playing business leaders and politicians has helped me no end. Before I make that telephone call, or walk into that meeting I remind myself how human they are and then go for it. It works wonders every time.

ACTION: Who are the people who cause you to self-doubt? What could you imagine them doing that would transform the way you think about them?

Part B: Keep Relationships

Keeping your relationships alive

Secret 38: Follow through or fail

There was a time when I met someone at an event who interested me greatly. I was keen to keep in touch and continue to get to know him, so – as always – I wrote to him after the event to ask for an initial meeting. He said no. I put a date in my diary for six months later, and when the diary note popped up, I asked again. He said no again, this time because he was travelling overseas. Six months later another diary note prompted me to get in touch again, asking for a meeting a third time. He said yes and invited me to lunch.

Over the years, I have found that people will often reject an initial meeting because they are very busy, yet I also suspect that it can be a bit of a test to see how interested we are in meeting. Most people give up with the first rejection.

Whenever I meet someone at an event that I would like to stay in contact with, I always drop them a note afterwards. I set myself a personal target of when I will contact them, normally within twenty-four to forty-eight hours. Mostly it is to say I hope we can keep in contact, to send them information we discussed or, on other occasions, I suggest meeting to talk further. I have learnt that unless you do this immediately after meeting with someone, they are likely to forget you, and you are likely to forget them. Besides keeping you in their memory, making contact again places your email address and other contact details permanently in their mail system.

What is the point of investing time, money and energy in going to events to meet people if we do nothing about reconnecting with them afterwards?

Our choice is simple – follow through or fail.

ACTION: Who have you failed to follow up with? Is there anything to lose by having a second or third go at keeping in contact?

Secret 39: Choose to be an initiator

There are two types of people in the world – imitators and initiators, and the former greatly outnumbers the latter. In fact, 95% of people imitate – following the crowd, resisting the temptation to strike out and do something bold and new – while only 5% will be proactive, deliberate initiators.

If we choose today to become an intentional, courageous initiator, we differentiate ourselves from the vast majority of others. But it costs us, and initiators face a daily challenge to break away from the pack. Will you make the extra phone call while others give up? Will you initiate lunch with a prospect or stick to a sandwich on your own? Will you act when others procrastinate?

That extra effort, grit and determination can make the difference between success and failure.

When I was in my early twenties I was invited to a dinner for young leaders. At the event there were a small number of experienced and seasoned leaders for us to rub shoulders with. One of them invited me to keep in touch with him after the event – I took him at his word and deliberately sought out a relationship with him. Over the years, he's become one of my most valued mentors and a long-standing friend, and I continue to see him on a regular basis.

These days I'm often at events where I know I'm going to meet lots of people. So before I even get to the venue, I think about being intentional in whom I build a relationship with as a result of the evening, and I'll be on the lookout for who that one person is.

ACTION: What's the next event on your calendar? Who might be there that you want to meet? How are you going to prepare for it?

Secret 40: Relationships are a contact sport

Relationships are a contact sport – 80% of relationship is simply staying in contact with another person.

This is what I call "pinging" – intentionally finding meaningful reasons to be in contact with someone.

It might sound obvious, but being in regular contact with people just makes relationships easier. Think about the times when you've met someone once and then you meet them again a year later. At worst they don't remember that they've even met you, while at best they might recall your face but won't have retained any details about who you are and what you do. You've neglected to develop the relationship and that means having to start again. The idea also applies to relationships that are more established – regular contact shows they are genuine while a lack of contact can lead the other person to doubt our motives for suddenly getting in touch.

There are obvious reasons like birthdays, wedding anniversaries and Christmas that help us keep in contact. Sometimes we can create personal anniversary events – like one employer I know who takes his PA out for lunch each year on their anniversary of working together. Small things like this really contribute to keeping a relationship alive.

There are also a myriad of other less obvious reasons to be in contact, and you don't even have to have a long conversation when you do touch base. When you talk on the telephone, set expectations straight away and say, 'This is just a quick call to…'

ACTION: Remember that every point of contact is an opportunity to strengthen our rapport and our relationships. Which of yours need a little time invested in them today?

Secret 41: Be attentive and adaptable

You and I will each build better interpersonal relationships if we are more attentive and adaptable.

The better we are at learning to read other people and altering our behaviour as a result, the greater the depth of connection we will make.

There are three key areas in which our attentiveness and adaptability can really come into their own:

Human need

If I think about a person out of the blue more than once I take it as a prompt to be in contact with them. It is amazing how many times that a hunch has connected me with a person at a critical moment in their life. Often this is as simple as sending someone an email only to receive one back that says, "I was just about to email you...". Or it's when I give someone a call and they tell me that I've phoned at exactly the right moment because they wanted to chat to me about something important.

Personality

The fact that we're all uniquely different makes for great variety and wealth in our relationships, but it also requires that we know how to read and respond to each other. For example, as an extrovert, I have learnt the importance of being attentive to people and situations, and knowing when to "turn the volume down" to avoid the risk of being insensitive to others. We need to be attentive to the personalities of other people and adapt accordingly.

Communication preferences

There are many different ways to communicate, and learning to spot – and then use – another person's preferences will add great value to your relationship. For example, I have one friend who uses snail mail rather than email. It can be interesting when it comes to scheduling a time to meet, but valuing him means interacting with him in a way that feels comfortable. Get to know the communication preferences for each person in your network, you might even like to make a note on your database, particularly if it is someone you are in contact with less often.

Being attentive and adaptable allows relationships to be established in a way that is most natural for the other person. Whether they notice it or not, allowing a relationship to function on their terms makes them feel more at ease and more able to be themselves.

ACTION: Who do you need to be more adaptable with this week? Make up your mind to be more attentive and adaptable.

Secret 42: Never take non-responsiveness personally

You go to the event, meet lots of people, but there's one person that you feel as though you have made a special connection with. The next day you send them an email, saying that it would be great to meet for coffee and chat further. No response. Nothing at all. It's all too easy to take this silence personally or to read it as "I'm not interested". I would encourage you to think differently.

In the first year of getting to know someone who I'm now in very close relationship with, I had to choose to either be patient and persist, or give up on the relationship altogether. The first few times we tried to meet, he cancelled our appointments, and was regularly over an hour late for subsequent meetings. But because I was intrigued by him and keen to know more about his world, I persevered and made adjustments for him. Later, I discovered there was an extremely difficult family situation that was causing these behaviours. Today we continue to be great friends.

People we've just met, or even those we've known for a while, will not always respond to an email, text or phone call. It's good to remind ourselves of the fact that we never know what might be going on in their life at that moment. We should try and put ourselves in their shoes. Perhaps they are under immense pressure at work – they might be doing the annual accounts, preparing for a pitch, attending a conference, reporting to the board the following day, or their job or business may be under threat. Or it could be that things are busy at home with a newborn child, a sick relative, a stressed partner, a house move, or holiday preparations.

We need to give people the benefit of the doubt.

My approach is to leave one message, then after that, phone until I get them personally. I don't leave further messages, doing so would only put them under more pressure. After all, there is a difference between being persistent and being overly pushy. When eventually you get to speak and meet, people will be really grateful that you didn't give up.

ACTION: List all those people with whom you've given up making contact. Pick one and commit to getting in touch with them again.

Secret 43: Respond don't react

This principle is one that I've learnt from bitter experience. If someone we know acts out of character – or someone we don't know behaves irrationally – we shouldn't react. The reality is that relationships aren't easy. Everyone is human, so there will always be instances when we will upset other people or other people upset us.

There are times when I've received an email that's really annoyed me and I've reacted badly, rattling off an instant reply and hitting send. Often this has made the situation much worse rather than improving it. Instead, a considered response is better.

Often, using a different medium, such as picking up the phone instead of emailing back, diffuses the situation.

There are three classic ways people react:

Fight

One reaction is to go into battle mode and tell people exactly what we think. Reacting like this may make us feel better immediately, but it will escalate the situation.

Flight

Another reaction is to run away and completely avoid the situation. This may provide temporary respite but the circumstances will not be resolved and may get worse by simply running away from them.

Freeze

A third reaction is to freeze like a rabbit caught in the headlights, choosing not to acknowledge the situation at all. Reacting in this way may mean the situation does not get worse – unless you are a rabbit – but again it will not resolve anything.

Putting these three classic reactions aside I would recommend the following response: Pause. Hold your breath. Think carefully about what might possibly be going on in the person's life to cause them to behave like this, and even if nothing is apparent, give them some slack. Then make a measured response.

Sometimes we will react rather than respond. When we do, we will need to practice the art of repairing relationships. This often comes down to our human capacity to apologise and also to forgive. If we can eat humble pie from time to time, we will find ourselves keeping relationships rather than losing them.

ACTION: How do you want to react the next time someone mistreats you? When you're feeling calm and rational, write a note on your phone that describes the kind of response you'd like to exhibit. Next time you feel the urge to react, read the note, pause and then respond.

Keeping in contact with everyone you know

Secret 44: A handful of soul mates

A client once asked me how I keep in contact with everyone I know. I told them I have a system. They looked perplexed.

I admit that the thought of having a system for relationships may sound like an oxymoron. How can you put human relationships into a management system?

I believe that relationships are too important to leave to chance, so I develop ways of trying to keep connected.

At the heart of my system are my soul mates. They are the people I talk to about anything and everything because I trust them completely. These are my closest friends and confidants to whom I show my unedited self. If I asked you to name your soul mates right now you could probably do so without hesitation.

People rarely, if ever, have more than a single handful of soul mates. The intimacy – emotionally and psychologically – we have with these people means that on average we have, at most, three to five people at this level of relationship. Most of our conversations in life are with our closest five relationships. The marketing consultancy Keller Faye found that 27% of our conversations are with our spouse/partner,

25% are with another family member and 10% are with a best friend. So who are your nearest and dearest?

ACTION: Who are your soul mates? Show them some appreciation today.

Secret 45: Programme your speed dial

In Secret 44 I told you about my soul mates and mentioned the fact that I have a system for keeping contact with all the people that I know. That system is built on the idea of the relationships falling into one of five concentric circles, with my soul mates at the very heart of the action.

Taking a step back to the next circle, I have about fifty people who I have most frequent contact with, possibly daily, weekly or most certainly monthly. I call them my speed diallers, as they're the ones I've programmed into the fifty quick dial slots I have on my phone. They may be colleagues, clients, friends, family and neighbours.

Most days I will read down the list of names on my speed dial list, using it as a prompt to see who I need to be in contact with.

Who would make it onto your list?

ACTION: Update your speed dial list today.

Secret 46: Write a Christmas card list

People vary in their propensity for relationships. One of my friends says that he can only cope with a handful – and by that he means literally five – of relationships at any one time. Another friend has hundreds of strong relationships all over the world. It doesn't matter where you are going or what you are doing, there is always someone he wants to introduce you to.

Over the years I have come to understand that each person has a different relational bandwidth for human relationships. That capacity for relationships is influenced by a range of variable factors, including:

Personality type e.g. introvert or extrovert
Profession e.g. sales or research
Life purpose e.g. fame or solitude
Geographic context e.g. rural or urbanite

Professor Robin Dunbar of the University of Oxford is best known for his research about the "cognitive limit to the number of individuals with whom any one person can maintain stable relationships". Dunbar developed a range for the number of stable relationships which stretched from 100 to 230 with an average of 150.

Let's make this practical. You probably have a Christmas card list tucked away somewhere. Perhaps it's a dedicated section on your database that you use for e-cards, or a traditional address book from which you write addresses on envelopes. These are people who have been significant in your life and you are committed to not losing contact with them. The number of people on that list may well be within Dunbar's range.

My Seasonal Greetings circle is the community of relationships that make up my third group.

I don't only use this list at Christmas, as each month I look at the names to remind myself of who really matters to me and who I need to be in contact with.

ACTION: If you don't have one yet it might well be time to write a Christmas card list, whatever time of year it is. Try it today.

Secret 47: Optimise social media

Social media provides us with the ability to engage with unprecedented numbers of people. At the time of writing Facebook has more than 1 billion users, LinkedIn over 200 million and Twitter over 140 million. The variety of other social media platforms specialising in different mediums continue to multiply. Together, they help us to keep connected with people we know but also people we are interested in knowing.

There are a couple of thousand people with whom I am connected to through social media that I know well. These I would describe as strong ties. By contrast there are tens of thousands of others who connect with me online because they are interested in what I do and want to know more, but I do not know them. I would describe these as weak ties. This is my social media network and the fourth circle of relationships.

New business focuses on building strong ties or close relationships with a defined group of prospects. However the value of the weak ties or superficial relationships should not be underestimated in the new business process. There are many times when the next piece of new business does not emerge from the strong ties but from the weaker ones. Out of the blue you hear from a contact you met once or twice many years ago, but who has been tracking you on social media, and now has a piece of work they would like you to do.

One of the big benefits of social media is that it allows

you to build a network of weak tie relationships that can in time provide a critical layer of new business opportunities.

ACTION: What does your use of social media say about you? Would you like it to tell a better story? Make a start this week.

Secret 48: Believe the world is your oyster

When was the last time someone declined the opportunity to meet you? Last week? Last month? A year ago? In my opinion, the more recent the better! If you haven't been turned down for a meeting recently, then perhaps you aren't reaching out to meet new people enough. Perhaps you're giving in to the temptation to create a risk-free environment of safe relationships, rather than expecting to meet a constant stream of new people.

My fifth circle of relationships is society at large, because I believe wholeheartedly in the value of the saying "the world is your oyster". Remember the notion of six degrees of separation – how each of us is only a friend of a friend of a friend of a friend of a friend away from knowing anybody at all on this planet. There is no single person on this planet that we cannot meet if we really want to.

Everyone has the potential to be within our relationship circle.

ACTION: Perhaps now is the time to take a risk and reach out. Who is out there in the global village that you would really like to meet, but have not yet tried to interact with?

Building your personal brand

Secret 49: Be your own brand

I recently purchased a new bicycle for my wife. She was drawn to the striking pink colour scheme and the seat that looked as comfortable as an armchair, while I fell for the little enamel badge that was attached to the front. It belonged to a brand that oozed the classic English manufacturing values of elegance and trustworthiness.

Branding goes a lot further than bikes and phones, and there's even a case for suggesting that each of us is our own personal brand. According to international business guru Tom Peters, our most important job is to be head marketer for the brand called you. Whether you are a corporate career executive or a high risk entrepreneur, building your personal brand – creating, maintaining and communicating the essence of what you are about – is one of the critical components in your success. It may help you to consider your own brand by asking the following three questions:

What is it you do better than anyone else you know?
What do you want people to say about you when you are not in the room?
What is it that people actually say about you when you are not in the room?

The greater the alignment between the answers to these questions, the stronger your personal brand.

We constantly make decisions about other people based on the impressions they make on us. Everything from their work environment to their attire, their handshake to their conversational style, they all collide and combine to create an impression. And this is great news for you; by recalibrating the way you think, speak, write, dress and listen, you can dramatically change almost everything about how people perceive you.

ACTION: Ask someone you know and trust to help you think through the three core questions in this secret – and do the same for them.

Secret 50: Be your own publisher

In a previous career I ran a business hosting fine food and wine events for corporate clients. To help me build my personal brand I began publishing a blog "London Dining Guides". I wrote about the best hotels, restaurants and bars to visit in the capital, posting articles on anything from roof top restaurants and alfresco dining to guides to the best place to get a great English afternoon tea and which table to ask for in which restaurant.

It worked! The blog helped me establish my personal brand for knowing food, wine and venues. Business leaders would contact me to ask advice about where to dine for various occasions, they would book me to host important client dinners and more and more people signed up for the blog.

There are so many advantages to blogging. With services like Wordpress it's free, easy and gives you the power to publish whatever you like, whenever you like.

But how do you create a successful blog?

Create quality content providing added value to the people you want to read it.
Develop a striking blog format e.g. attention-grabbing title, engaging story, image, main point, bullet point, closing question, author, social media buttons, comments.
Publish series of blog postings, rather than one-offs.
Build an email list of people who are interested in your blog using a provider such as AWeber or MailChimp.
Signpost people to your blog from every possible source

including email newsletters, Twitter, LinkedIn, Facebook, Google+

Never has it been easier to build your public profile.

You no longer need to beg and grovel with the traditional newspapers and magazines for the smallest mention of you, your product or your service. The potential is limitless.

ACTION: Take time to search out a couple of bloggers that are creating content that inspires and equips you.

Secret 51: Be your own broadcaster

Twitter allows us to build our personal brand in unique ways.

How to do it? I'd start by covering these basics:

Get a great head shot photo for your profile (and add a background image).
Craft a profile bio that gives credibility and creates human interest.
Start blogging regularly and consistently.
Pre-schedule social media posts to provide consistency and regularity (e.g. Buffer).
Engage with people and be generous in promoting, retweeting and following others.

Thanks to a couple of strategies that I used, my Twitter following has grown from under 1,000 people to over 10,000 people in less than a year.

* When I speak to a group of people, whether large or small, I invite them to switch on their phones (but leave them on silent), follow me on Twitter and tweet about my speech. I have had as much as 75% of an audience respond positively to this invitation. Of course the results vary depending on the demographics of the audience. For example in West Africa I invite people to "Like" me on Facebook because that is the prominent social media platform in that market.

* The second factor that has had the greatest impact on

boosting my Twitter following is by leveraging the law of reciprocation. Simply put, it means that people desire to give back in the same way that they have received. If you follow someone on Twitter there is a likelihood they will reciprocate and follow you back. Identify your gurus, follow who is following them and wait for the law of reciprocation to play out.

ACTION: Next time you speak somewhere invite people to switch their mobile phones on – silent – follow you and tweet about your speech.

Secret 52: Selling etiquette

People buy you before they buy your product. Your personal likability, knowability and trustability are vital players in the buying process. Your product may be the best on the market, but if people don't like, know and trust you they won't buy. And if you're in a service-based business these influences are even more accentuated.

So how do you sell yourself effectively? There are three approaches to authentic selling:

The straight sell

Be up front and explain that you've an "opportunity" you would like to discuss. Once you have presented the opportunity and discussed it you are free to try and close a sale.

The subtle sell

Be intentional and relaxed about mentioning the story of one of your current client assignments. It is critical this is understood as simply a story and not a pitch. You may well be asked questions, however if you are not, move on.

The no-sell sell

Be completely yourself in building a non-transactional relationship. Talk about business in a natural way. If there is a time when your product or service is relevant you will be asked more about it.

It is of critical importance in selling etiquette that both motivation and expectations are completely transparent.

Each of the approaches above has 100% integrity.

ACTION: What kind of salesperson are you? The chances are that one of the above will be a favourite, but don't let that stop you from trying the other two. Have a go at experimenting with different techniques.

Being courageous in your relationships

Secret 53: Be your unedited self

I was young when I last took part in a theatrical production. I had to dress up as an historical figure and recite from memory extracts from their journal. I relished the challenge of committing such large chunks of text to memory, and delivering them with gusto was never going to be a problem for me. But the costume was a different story. It was profoundly uncomfortable and deeply embarrassing. The only positive was that the costume was so elaborate that very few people recognised me.

Most of us are more comfortable being ourselves rather than acting as someone else. However, being your true and authentic self requires courage. I call it being your "unedited self", and it requires you to be vulnerable, to take a risk, trusting that other people will accept you for who you really are.

Being your unedited self won't only change the way that people respond to you, it will change the way that you respond to them.

In time, with the confidence that comes from vulnerability, you might find yourself encouraging others to be equally unedited when you:

Ask a penetrating question
Provide challenging feedback

Make or invite a self disclosure
Raise an area of interpersonal conflict

Until we are courageous we can only ever speculate about whether others are willing to reciprocate and be as equally bold as us. In other words, if we want our relationships to go deeper, one of us is going to have to make the first move and stop hiding behind the mask. What's stopping you from this level of freedom?

ACTION: Aim to have one conversation today in which you are at your risk-taking, unedited best.

Secret 54: Don't give it a second thought

Every now and again I'll become taken with a new interest. A few years ago I went game shooting with a friend and enjoyed it so much that I decided to learn to shoot. I started by taking up clay pigeon shooting, and immersed myself in the myriad technical things to learn, from the way the gun worked, the methods of ensuring safety and the correct technique for mounting the gun. I learned strange new terms and rhymes to help me stick to the correct sequence, and before long I was "killing the bird", "sweeping through the bird" and mastering the "bum, beak, bang" approach.

As I became a more and more proficient "gun", I learnt not to think about the process. I discovered that the "birds" that I failed to kill were the ones where I thought too much about what I was doing. If I thought too much about how I was standing, the way the gun was mounted, the sight, or anything other than the "bird", I would invariably hesitate and miss.

Now, sometimes it is right that we take our time and remember the essential steps for a good technique. But often – in business, relationships and clay pigeon shooting alike – we hesitate at our peril. A range of negative thoughts can circle above us, preventing us from believing in ourselves and our abilities.

Lack of self-belief
Lack of relational confidence
Fear of failure
Fear of rejection

Deep insecurity
Desire to play it safe

Sometimes all of the above can drown out our ability to think straight. We have to try and turn down or silence the noise that they create.

We have to choose to be courageous.

We must strike the balance between hesitation and impetuousness. Get it wrong and we risk being either inactive or foolish. Get it right and we find courage and confidence that can benefit not only us, but our business and clients.

ACTION: Don't hesitate today.

Secret 55: Build your inner legitimacy

Once a year, the community where my family and I live becomes the focal point of the world when it hosts the Wimbledon Lawn Tennis Championship. In 2013, the atmosphere was even better than ever as Andy Murray beat Novak Djokovic in the final.

The skill on display was incredible. The physical strength and stamina was outstanding. Spectacular courage was displayed by each player, and the world looked on in awe.

Where do you find the courage to play the game of life? Factors that may contribute to your confidence include:

Position in your field of expertise and in life
Personal and organisational brand
Support of clients, colleagues and coaches as well as family and friends
Financial freedom and freedom from worry
Education, skills training and preparation
Physical fitness and stamina
Appearance and how you dress
Your world view and belief system

Murray and Djokovic certainly drew strength from each of these external resources, however there was something much deeper going on. As the infamous book *The Inner Game of Tennis* explains, it is the non-external factors that largely determine sporting performance. This is what I describe as your "inner legitimacy", the degree to which you are comfortable, content and confident with who you are.

Classically, this inner authority is developed by spending time by yourself away from the distractions of life. In this place you can quieten your mind and visualise what success looks like.

"Inner legitimacy" is tested when the external supports fail you.

Inner legitimacy is challenged when this happens, and is the point at which you discover where your real strength comes from – whether from your external props or your inner authority.

ACTION: Schedule some time to be with yourself so that you can work on your inner legitimacy and play to win.

Secret 56: Exercise your courage muscles

Most of us have a special breed of friends and acquaintances who love the gym. You might be one yourself – the sort of person who puts time into getting your body toned the way you like it. Whatever you wear looks great on you, and the hard work is paying off.

Courage is one of the muscles that too few of us choose to exercise. Yet the more consistently you practise and exercise courage the stronger, fitter and more courageous you become. Conversely the less you exercise courage the more out of shape, lazy and fearful you become. As the gym instructors tell us, "muscles have memories". Courage is no different.

Think about the key people in your life, both professional and personal, and how you could be more courageous in your relationships with them. Could you:

Challenge them if they have become stagnant in their job
Offer some feedback about a way they could improve themselves
Make a self-disclosure/tell them something personal you've never said before
Ask what their greatest work challenge is and how you could help
Cross the boundaries of professional and personal life by meeting with partners

Becoming more courageous in your relationships does introduce an element of risk.

When you consider the best that could happen and worst that could happen as a result, exercising your courage muscles wins every time.

ACTION: Remember the truism that what you feed, grows. Feed your courage today by doing something bold and brave in a relationship.

Repairing damaged relationships

Secret 57: Heartfelt recognition

Just recently it came to my attention that someone with whom I thought I had a good relationship was actually offended by me. What made the situation more difficult was that they hadn't told me – I had discovered it through a third party.

Regardless of how you find out or who may be to blame, the first step towards repairing relationships is heartfelt recognition that you have offended the other person.

Somehow, you need to find words to genuinely and authentically recognise that you have offended.

"Please tell me how I have offended you"
"I realise I have offended you"
"I have wronged you, please tell me more"

Words like these provide the opportunity for the offended party to let you know what you did, or didn't do. It lets them know that you want to know how it impacted them and that you are inviting them to speak while you listen intently, ask questions sensitively and try to understand as fully as possible what has gone wrong.

Whether you think the other person is justified in being offended, or whether you think you are innocent is actually irrelevant.

If someone is offended by you, you need to know about it and you need to act. Heartfelt recognition is the first step in repairing relationships.

ACTION: Who do you need to go to today and acknowledge that something has gone wrong?

Secret 58: Take responsibility

The student common room was hired out for a party. It was now midnight and the music was thumping through every floor of the college. Requests had been made to turn the music down, but still the party continued. When all attempts at reason failed, there was only one course of action available; cutting the power. Instantly the music died, and almost as instantly the disgruntled party revellers headed home in complete darkness.

You can imagine what headlined the agenda at that week's community meeting. Things got worse when it became clear that the college caretaker kept tropical fish, and due to the lack of power to the water pump that night there had been a fatality in the fish tank. The pressure was on and the game was up. Somebody needed to own up to flicking the switch. Since I'd been the one to cut the power, I confessed to the crime.

Most offences – even ones that result in the death of much loved marine life – are not malicious. Most offences are genuine mistakes with unintended consequences. Yet whatever the intentions, communicating clearly that you are taking responsibility is essential:

"I was wrong"
"I have offended you"
"I know I have let you down"
"I have hurt you"
"It was my mistake"

There can be no avoidance, no wriggling, no passing the buck and no excuses, no pointing the finger of blame elsewhere. The offence needs to be owned.

Taking responsibility is the second critical step on the pathway of repairing relationships that have gone wrong.

ACTION: What mistake do you need to take responsibility for?

Secret 59: Express regret

There was a prospective client that I had been slowly working towards securing a contract with. They left their day book at an event I was hosting and so I ended up carrying it around with me for several days. Eventually I decided it wasn't needed and got fed up carrying it so I recycled it! Within half an hour my prospective client's PA was on the telephone wanting to send a courier to collect the day book because it was very important.

Rarely have I felt more culpable than I did in this moment. I immediately telephoned my prospective client to explain what had happened and expressing regret. As it turned out that same telephone call also resulted in the confirmation to do business together.

Ensuring that the offended party knows of your remorse is fundamental in moving on from the past to the future:

"I am sorry"
"I apologise"
"I regret what has happened"
"Please forgive me"

There is no way out, if you have upset, hurt or offended someone, nothing less than a sincere and full apology will suffice.

Offering an apology may well be one of the toughest business decisions you have to make today. Professional advisers are meant to be right so admitting the opposite is a tough call.

However, when you do it demonstrates integrity and trustworthiness and is likely to lead to more business not less. Expressing regret is the third step in the process of repairing relationships.

ACTION: Who do you need to say sorry to today?

Secret 60: Make restitution

Middle age has truly arrived in the Bird family. Recently we have taken on the tenancy of an allotment, and the whole family is excited by it. In fact, we've been so keen that we had a whole stack of railway sleepers delivered so that we could build a raised bed for each of the children to call their own. The flatbed lorry duly delivered the sleepers and headed off, but little did we know that the driver decided to take the long route out of the allotment, got stuck in the mud and left four colossal holes in the path where no holes should be – making the track virtually impassable for other users. When we finally did discover what had happened, we were mortified and so made apology to the chair of the allotment association. In addition we headed off with our spades to repair the mud track which had been left with four big pot holes.

Words are cheap unless they are accompanied by action. The words "I am sorry, please forgive me" are relatively easy to say. Putting things right is harder to do. Sometimes it is obvious what the act of making restitution can be and on other occasions we need to ask:

"How can I put things right?"
"What can I do to make it better?"
"How can I restore the situation?"
"What is the best way to repair the relationship?"

A verbal apology may mean swallowing our pride, but to repair the relationship or restore the situation to what it was before it was broken is a tougher assignment.

Yet the act of putting things right can sometimes lead to greater trust and a stronger relationship. Making restitution is the fourth dimension of repairing relationships.

ACTION: How can you put right today a mistake you have made?

Secret 61: Offer reassurance

My wife and I are happily married, yet over the years there are ways that I have consistently upset her. The fact that I am a repeat offender in various ways makes it harder and harder to apologise, but part of the value of strong relationships is helping someone to change over a long period of time.

Most of us have habitual behaviours that other people struggle with.

Our bad habits are particularly difficult for those people who are closest to us because they experience them most frequently and intensely. Yet just because we struggle to break away from them it doesn't absolve us of the responsibility of offering reassurance when we offend:

"It won't happen again"
"I will try my very best not to do that again"
"I am a work in progress"
"Will you help me change?"

The sobering challenge for us all is to consider that it's not only how we can avoid repeating behaviour that offends people but how we can reassure them of our positive intentions for the future. A commitment to avoid doing something again is the fifth and final dimension of repairing relationships.

ACTION: Who do you need to offer reassurance to today?

Overcoming the fear of failure

Secret 62: Believe anything is possible

At its best, the fear of failure can cause you to lower both your life aspirations and expectations. At its worst, the fear of failure can leave you paralysed, inactive and unable to break out. It is a completely human response and an understandable way of trying to protect yourself from the pain of failure. Yet if we allow the fear of it to get out of hand, we can be headed for real trouble.

'The tragedy in life doesn't lie in not reaching your goal. The tragedy lies in having no goal to reach.'
Benjamin Mays

'I can accept failure, everyone fails at something. But I can't accept not trying.'
Michael Jordan

When you know freedom from fear of failure you can raise your hopes, aim high and set audacious goals, regardless of the possibility and consequences of failure. When you are free from the fear of failure you live in a place where you believe anything is possible – because it is.

Failure is inevitable; why not fail while aiming at something worthwhile?

ACTION: Ask yourself this question: if I was completely

fearless what goals would I set for myself? If you are serious about having a go write down:

What would I like to be?
What would I like to do?
What would I like to have?

Secret 63: Keep on keeping on

The fear of failure can lead you to action paralysis – which is when your anxiety about what is before you causes you to freeze up and stop trying. Sometimes you are unable to grasp the next opportunity and challenge in life, because you have not overcome your last experience of failure.

'The difference between success and failure is the ability to get up and start again.'
Winston Churchill

'The man who does not make mistakes is unlikely to make anything.'
English Proverb

'If you fell down yesterday, stand up today.'
H. G. Wells

When you are free from the fear of failure you have attained a higher level of self-control and self-mastery. You have determined that you will not make a friend of fear but you will live in a place of liberty where you have decided you will never give up trying. Ask yourself how you can dig deep in yourself to keep on keeping on, even when you have failed.

Failure is inevitable; why not fail with freedom?

ACTION: If you are serious about never giving up ask:

What internal resources can I draw upon?

What team/organisational resources can I draw upon?
What environmental resources can I draw upon?

Secret 64: Fail well

Most of us would rather turn away from fear. We shut the door on spiders and turn the lights on when the movie gets too much. But while these are fine reactions for certain situations, turning a blind eye to our fear of failure is a mistake. By ignoring it, we deny ourselves the opportunity of getting the one good thing that failure offers us – some of the most vital life lessons of all.

There is more to learn from the pain of failure than the pleasures of success. Success offers sanitised learning, however failure produces real life, gritty personal change and transformation.

'It's fine to celebrate success but it is more important to heed the lessons of failure.'
Bill Gates

'Failure is simply the opportunity to begin again, this time more intelligently.'
Henry Ford

'So why do I talk about the benefits of failure? Simply because failure meant a stripping away of the inessential.'
J K Rowling

When you are free from the fear of failure you can learn how to fail well and fail forward. You can decide that failure will make you a better person rather than a bitter person. You can commit to extracting every ounce of learning from your failures in order to move forward and improve yourself.

Failure is inevitable; why not fail better next time?

ACTION: Ask yourself, how could you be changed for the better through your most recent experience of failure? If you are serious about self-improvement consider:

What can I learn from myself?
What can I learn from my trusted friends and advisers?
What can I learn from my critics? (This requires the most courage and the most discernment, however it can provide you with another dimension.)

Secret 65: Get perspective

The fear of failure can cause us to lose perspective. We give more attention to the worst possible outcomes than we do to the best possible scenarios. We see failure as final rather than temporary. Yet we are wrong.

'Success isn't permanent and failure isn't fatal, it is the courage to continue that counts.'
Winston Churchill

'I didn't fail the test, I just found 100 ways to do it wrong.'
Benjamin Franklin

When you are free from the fear of failure you have a unique life perspective. Failure changes from a tombstone to a stepping stone to your future. Failure changes from becoming your undertaker to becoming your teacher. Freedom from the fear of failure is a mindset which we choose to adopt above all else, that battles for the attention and energy of our heart and mind.

Failure is inevitable; why not fail with perspective?

ACTION: Ask yourself the question 'How am I giving the fear of failure a power in my life that it should not have?' If you are serious about changing your perspective reflect:

How can I change my mindset and attitudes?
How can I change my values and beliefs?
How can I change my habits and behaviours?

Secret 66: Be peaceful

The fear of failure means we can live our life dominated with anxiety about tomorrow. We are robbed of living in the moment and of seizing today's opportunities. We become increasingly focused on self-preservation and less attentive to the people around us.

'Worry does not empty tomorrow of its sorrow; it empties today of its strength.'
Corrie Ten Boom

'A man can fail many times, but he isn't a failure until he begins to blame somebody else.'
John Burroughs

'Fear doesn't exist anywhere except in the mind.'
Dale Carnegie

When you are free from the fear of failure, you can quieten your mind, suspend mental self-instruction and be completely present in the moment, regardless of what is going on around you. You are liberated to be your authentic, unedited self through both glorious success or glorious failure.

Failure is inevitable; why not be at peace with yourself?

ACTION: Ask yourself what would be the worst that would happen if you actually did fail. If you are serious about becoming a peaceful, successful person, take time out today to:

Be comfortable in your own skin
Develop your mental strength
Consider if you need to change the way you are thinking
about your situation

Part C: Grow Relationships

Growing your relationships

Secret 67: Say what you do and do what you say

When you buy a new product you 'expect it to do what it says on the tin' otherwise you don't buy it again. When you are promised a level of customer service but don't experience it, you vote with your feet. When someone says they will do something for you, you expect them to do it otherwise there is a loss of trust.

It is relatively easy to say what you do, but it is so much harder to do what you say. Consistency is one of the most important attributes of any relationship because it grows trust, establishes reliability and increases the desire to work together. Contrastingly inconsistency erodes trust and questions integrity.

Integrity is what we do when no one is looking.

Integrity is doing the right thing regardless of the consequences. Integrity is what we say about a person when they are not in the room. Relational integrity means seeing the best in people, always saying the best about people and always doing the best for people. It means being transparent and honest.

ACTION: What relationships and situations do you need to have a little more integrity in?

Secret 68: Give to grow, don't give to get

The value of most of the goods we purchase in life decreases the moment we take ownership. Perhaps the most renowned depreciating asset is the new car, which loses thousands of pounds the very minute it's driven out of the showroom. Relationships, on the other hand, are different. Relationships are appreciating assets. Relationships are an investment – if we nurture and protect them they will last a lifetime and continue to appreciate in value.

Someone once told me about a relationship mantra they had heard; "give to get". I didn't like it. It sounded shallow, short term and selfish – networking at its worst.

Authentic relationships are founded on the principle of "give to grow". It's not about what we get in a relationship, it's about what we are able to give. There will undoubtedly be benefits in every relationship, but a genuine one is not founded solely on these things. There will be times when we give to a relationship and times when we will receive from it. The critical point is that we are in the relationship for the long game, not primarily for what we get out of it.

When we give to grow the long-term value of relationships, we do not give to get short-term gain.

When a relationship has longevity, it changes and transforms both parties for the better. So play the long game.

ACTION: How long is your long game? Think about your

relationships and consider which of them span a decade or more. And who has been a constant force for good in your life for years? Thank them today.

Secret 69: Under promise and over deliver

Every time I enter my favourite restaurant I am greeted by name and shown to my usual table (number 32). I've been dining there for over a decade and so the waiter shows me to my preferred side of the table. Having sat down, iced water is poured into my glass and I look at the menu and make my selections. Chef sends an *amuse-bouche* to the table which whets my appetite for the three courses that are to follow. At the end of the meal they bring me a plate of my favourite petit fours as they know I don't like coffee but rather like the chocs.

The restaurant in question has mastered the art of offering all you would expect from a place of its kind, and then exceeding all expectations. Diners like me are continually impressed and keen to return.

Under-promise and over-deliver is a simple enough motto to remember, and putting it into practice will transform the way you relate to people.

ACTION: The first step to exceeding a customer's expectations is to know what those expectations are. How well do you know what your customers and clients expect of you?

Secret 70: Notice the small things

When we are doing big deals we can begin to think that the small things are not important. However, the people who grow lasting relationships understand that in life as well as business, the small things really are the big things.

Remembering a client's birthday, special holiday or that they have a sick family member shows that you've not only listened, but you have also made the effort to remember and respond appropriately.

Remembering where someone likes to eat, how they like to communicate or what mode of working they prefer might seem small in comparison to getting the deal done, but we ignore the small at our peril.

Remember!

ACTION: Before you eat your next meal, do something kind that shows you've thought about someone you value.

Secret 71: Never eat alone

A while ago I met a guy at a charity fundraising event and sent him an email afterwards saying it would be good to keep in contact. We did and, several months later, I dropped him a note to say I was going to be in the vicinity of his office and could I offer him a spot of lunch. We ate, drank and talked about everything possible, except doing business together. As we were about to leave the restaurant, he said that I ought to become his preferred supplier. This was completely unexpected, entirely surprising yet very pleasing. Such is the power of lunch.

Perhaps it wasn't entirely down to the risotto, but you get my point; the table is an almost magical place.

The table fosters intimacy and allows conversation to flow naturally. No wonder dating couples go out for dinner – sitting face to face, sharing the experience, it's almost impossible to eat with someone and not get to know them a little better.

We all have to eat, so why not cultivate the habit of taking meals – whether breakfast, lunch or dinner – with people with whom you want to grow and enrich your relationship.

ACTION: Who do you want to share a meal with this month? Book it up.

Secret 72: Learn reciprocity

When we return generosity with generosity, or a gift with a gift, or appreciation with appreciation, we are putting into action one of the most fundamental laws of human nature: we reap what we sow.

Relationships are about giving, and there's a natural two-way flow which is found in all the best ones.

Writing in his book *Enchantment*, Guy Kawasaki, formerly the chief technology evangelist for Apple, describes three reasons for reciprocity:

> Quid pro quo
>
> This is a mutual exchange, perhaps a formal contract, of goods for money or a psychological contract of help for help. This is giving with the expectation of receiving in return.
>
> Pay it forward
>
> This describes giving something with no immediate benefit or indeed without any actual guarantee of future benefit or reciprocity. This is giving with the hope that the recipient will in turn choose to be generous to others.
>
> Intrinsic reasons
>
> This is being generous for the sake of it, with

absolutely no expectation and often no possibility of being rewarded in turn. This is giving simply for the sake of giving.

ACTION: Who could you do something for today? Perhaps there is someone who is highly unlikely to be able to pay you back. Grow relationships with people around you by being generous regardless of any return on the relationship.

Secret 73: Do something together

Doing something with another person is a powerful way of growing a relationship. It actually doesn't matter how small the something is, after all, many big partnerships started out as a small experiments. Partnering on a small project has three advantages:

Test recalibration of relationship

We develop a good mode of working together. Making the transition from knowing and liking one another to working together takes time and effort, and requires a certain degree of recalibration of our relationship. Starting small allows those changes to evolve without the added pressure of too much expectation.

Test ways of working

As individuals with our own way of doing things we need to be aware of the fact that our own experiences and assumptions might not tally with our partner's. We will need to agree on and develop a new way of working together.

Test for benefit

If we partner on a small project and there is no benefit or little in the way of positive outcome, then it is easier to wind down a small project than a large one. However, if things are working very well then we can progress towards bigger opportunities.

So much of the above is about who we are and how we relate to others.

If we get it right once, what's to stop us from achieving far greater success in the future?

ACTION: Who do you want to partner with? When are you going to have the conversation that moves your plans on to the next stage?

Secret 74: Triangulate relationships

Triangulation is about growing a relationship by introducing two people we know in such a way that it creates mutual benefit. We might also gain from the introduction – perhaps receiving a commercial introducer's fee – but at other times the only payback for ourselves is the knowledge that we managed to play a part in forming a new partnership.

In every introduction, a transfer of trust takes place between the introducer and the person who is introduced (see Secret 9). Recommend a rogue lawyer to a client, and you risk damaging your own relationship. However, if your recommendations are good, clients are far more likely to listen to you in future.

Depending on the relationship between the introducer and the introduced, different levels of trust transfer can be utilised.

Trust transfer ranges from Level 1 for someone we don't know well, to Level 2 for someone we know, to Level 3 for someone we trust, to Level 4 for someone we are championing:

> Level 1 – A suggestion to talk to someone

> 'Tom, I think you should meet David.'

> Level 2 – Tell them to use your name

> 'Tom, please mention to David that I suggested you meet him.'

Level 3 – Introduce them by email

'Tom, I will email David introducing you and copy you in.'

Level 4 – Face to face meeting

'Tom, I'd like you to meet David, let me arrange a date for lunch.'

ACTION: Who could you introduce to someone else today? How are you going to introduce them?

Secret 75: Build your relational footprint

An executive I know was assigned to a client and told to grow the account which was already in the high seven figures. One dimension of the executive's strategy was to build his business's relational footprint within the client organisation. It all started slowly at first, but as he developed stronger and deeper relationships within the company, so did the number and value of his contracts.

Introduce and Refer

Initially, he asked the people he knew to introduce and refer him to other key stakeholders in the organisation.

Fluffy Edges

Secondly, he left fluffy edges around the meetings he had scheduled. Wherever possible he arrived in time for a cup of tea before the meeting and popped in to see someone afterwards. In this way he consistently made himself available.

Half Day

Finally, the client provided him with a security pass so he asked his secretary to begin blocking out a half day a week. This time was not structured, he would use it to walk the floor, bump into people in the canteen and be available to talk with.

When expanding your relational footprint, you must

be wary of – and sensitive to – internal politics.

Much of the key to managing politics is complete discretion and confidentiality, together with an approach of "no comment" and non-engagement.

ACTION: What kind of relational impression do you make on others? If you can't work it out for yourself, ask people you know and trust to help you see how others see you.

Secret 76: Create a network

Not everyone is an initiator (see Secret 39), but for those that are there's nothing quite as satisfying as creating a network. Perhaps you want to see the charities you support receive greater funding, or it might be that you can see several opportunities for people you know that are currently lying dormant. Whatever the reason, there are considerable benefits to being the person that draws others together with a common purpose:

Being perceived as a leader of leaders

You will become someone to whom others within your industry or sector look to for leadership. In addition, you and the members of the network will gradually develop a higher degree of insight and thought leadership.

Becoming a spokesperson

You and other senior network participants may experience increased opportunities to comment in the media, speak in public and even influence government thinking and policy.

Accelerating opportunities for yourself and others

You will accelerate the growth of the personal network of every participant and will therefore increase the opportunities open to them.

Starting a network is not for everyone. It requires catalytic leadership, unending motivation and a great propensity for investing in relationships.

If you think starting a network is for you, or could be for you, why not look for a need or opportunity and have a go. If you could start any network what would it be?

ACTION: If you don't want to start one, what are the networks out there that you want to join? Sign up today.

Shifting relationships that have become stale?

Secret 77: Make a self-disclosure

Each of us is a complicated and unique combination of experiences and assumptions. The Johari Window is a model for helping us better understand our relationship with ourselves as well as with others.

Imagine a house with four rooms, each one representing a different aspect of who we are:

The Public Room

This has big clear windows so that what is inside is known to us and others.

The Blind-Spot room

This room has windows that others can see through but they are at such an angle that we need others to hold up a mirror to enable us to see inside.

The Private Room

This has windows that we can see through, but we need to open them in order to allow others to see inside.

The Mystery Room

This has no windows and no doors, this room is full of the unknown, unconscious and subconscious.

The Private Room is the one that represents the hidden things about us, the things that we choose whether or not to disclose to others. This might be as simple as our age – I can think of several people who choose to not reveal how old they are – or it could be more intimate such as our fears.

Making a self-disclosure about the contents of your Private Room to a person sends the clear message that you trust them.

Self-disclosure will grow and enrich your relationship. You will often find that self-disclosure is reciprocated by the other person and a mutual exchange of trust takes place.

ACTION: Commit to going deeper in at least two conversations today.

Secret 78: Look for a critical friend

Within the Johari house (see Secret 77) there is the Blind-Spot Room. This room represents the things about us of which we are unaware, but others can see. Every single one of us has one.

How do you know what's in your Blind-Spot Room? Simple – you ask someone you trust to tell you. By inviting constructive feedback in this way you not only gain a greater degree of self-awareness, but you build trust between you.

Of course there will also be times when you must take courage and offer constructive feedback to someone else as well. Having invited someone to critique your own failings does wonders for your tact and sensitivity.

When you know what it feels like to have someone point out your blind spots, you're far more likely to be sensitive and thoughtful when pointing out another's.

ACTION: Who do you trust? Who trusts you? Spend time with them today.

Secret 79: Exercise trust

It was the school holidays, so my family and I did what we so often do and headed out for a day at a glorious National Trust property. But we weren't going for the country house – we were going for the space. My children craved the chance to run and shout without feeling we were disturbing the peace.

It was a beautiful day, and my four-year-old son Reuben climbed up onto an ancient wall, and ran along until he reached a pillar which he proceeded to climb. In seconds he was at the top, and with arms outspread shouted, 'Catch me Daddy!' and proceeded to launch himself into the air. In that millisecond I clicked out of holiday mode, adrenaline taking control of my functions. Despite having been a pretty poor catch at school, there was no way I was going to let my son come to any harm as he hurtled towards the ground.

I caught him and held him tight. I have never loved my son more. He knew that he could trust his dad, and our relationship became stronger as a result.

One of the ways that we can grow a relationship is by exercising trust in it.

I am not suggesting launching yourself from the vending machine into your CFO's arms, but take time to consider the other ways in which you might be able to demonstrate that you trust someone. Can you confide in them about some sensitive information, or rely on them to help with something critical to your business? Trust is a great currency within relationships. Why not spend some today?

ACTION: Take a relational risk today and see the way things change.

Secret 80: Celebrate together

There are many schools of thought when it comes to birthdays. Some like to let the years go by unmarked, others will celebrate significant milestones, and then there are people like me who like to do it large every year.

It is not uncommon for me to host two or three birthday celebrations each year. I use it as a great excuse to get together small groups of friends to simply enjoy one other. I gather small groups because I'm then able to spend time with each person. For my fortieth, I celebrated by taking a dozen friends on a weekend road trip to the champagne region. My experience is that these celebrations ensure people feel special and each year the relationship is enriched.

There are a couple of business owners I know who, each time they win a deal, buy a different bottle of champagne to celebrate together. They remove the label from the bottle and stick it in a book which records their deal flow. I know of a charity that works to rescue young people from dangerous situations, and whenever they have a success the whole team celebrates by opening a bottle of champagne.

Not all celebrations have to involve champagne, but it certainly helps!

ACTION: Celebrating creates a tangible feel-good factor that strengthens relationships. How can you find more excuses to celebrate with the people with whom you want to build stronger relationships?

Secret 81: Enjoy a shared interest

It is said that the best negotiators spend 40% of their preparation time finding shared interests with the other party. By finding some common ground we provide ourselves with an instant subject for conversation that accelerates interpersonal rapport and helps others to relax.

One of my favourite interests is fine dining, and over the years I have observed the ways in which my relationships have deepened with those with whom I share this passion. Whether it's updating our scorecards for our favourite restaurants or enjoying our annual port tasting event, when we share our passions with others, good things invariably flow as a result.

Shared interests are generally things from outside the immediate domain of the relationship.

If we are at work, a shared interest is likely to be something personal; if we are at home, it may include work. Shared interests can be a sport, hobby, politics, charity or family.

ACTION: Shared interests strengthen and enrich relationships. What are your passions and interests that you could potentially share with others?

Secret 82: Ask for help

It was a Saturday morning and I headed off on my bike with my bucket and sponge balanced on the handle bars. As a schoolboy I had started a modest car washing business, and it sure beat having a paper round and getting up at the crack of dawn seven days a week like the rest of my class mates.

The guy whose car I washed asked what I was going to do when I left school. I explained that I didn't know yet. He asked if it would help to apply for an apprenticeship with his business, I jumped at the opportunity. He helped me complete the application. He provided a reference. He helped me prepare for interview. And… I got a job! He continued to help me over the years by sponsoring me within the organisation. I wouldn't have got my first (and only ever) job without his help. Whatever our stage of life we all benefit from the help of others.

The offer of help

There's an entrepreneur I know who when I met him seemed to have everything. But he lacked a sense of what to do with his life. So I met with him on a regular basis, coached him and helped him develop a sense of purpose.

Take time to get to know other people's aims, aspirations and goals, then offer to help them achieve them.

Sign post to help

Leaders are always looking to work smarter, and to make life more simple and easy to manage. As you discover cutting edge smart phone apps, sources of knowledge or online services that you think are life-changing, point others towards them, especially if they save time or money.

The request for help

We can also ask for help from others. However, I would advise you to choose something that will be seen as no big deal to the person you are asking. They will feel great for helping you in a way that costs them little, and their little may be a lot to you.

Each of these "helps" will strengthen and enrich your relationships.

Offer help to people and occasionally ask for help yourself.

ACTION: Who do you know who needs your help right now? Give it to them, without reservation.

Secret 83: Talk about shared memories

A business entrepreneur was celebrating a special wedding anniversary and wanted it to be an occasion to remember. So he flew his family and friends to Spain for a weekend of celebrations that included a boat ride to a harbour side restaurant for dinner and pool side party. It was certainly a weekend to remember, and my friend and I still talk about it now.

Memories create strong relationships. My children love camping. When my son was five years old we slept in the garden shed overnight and cooked sausages and beans on the camping stove for our breakfast. Four years on and we still talk about this experience.

A charitable client and I created a high impact way to launch a public awareness campaign that involved a group of cross-party members of parliament building a slum and living in it for a couple of days, detoxing from their smart phones and living off of lentils. Again, it is a memory that we still talk about.

Creating memorable events and occasions is a powerful way to build our relationship with someone.

Sometimes the memorable event or the occasion is a difficult time that you got through together, a funny incident that took place or something that between you, you managed to pull off. It's about building a personal history that can be recalled in "do you remember the time we…" conversations.

ACTION: Think about some of your memories that involve the people you know best. How can you create further memories and enrich your relationships?

Building your business through referral relationships

Secret 84: Introductions verses referrals

When I first started out in business I remember the extraordinary generosity of a friend called Charlie. I had clarity about what I wanted to do, but I needed to find my first group of clients. Over lunch I was telling Charlie about my new venture and he immediately wanted to help. He made two offers.

The first offer was the invitation for me to visit his office and look through his address book. He offered to write a letter of introduction to whoever I selected – ambitiously I selected over fifty people.

Charlie also promised to make referrals for me to five people who he knew would benefit from my services. He explained he would speak to them and then email to introduce us.

This is when I learnt the difference between an "introduction" and a "referral":

Introduction

An opportunity to meet someone you might find interesting or you might be able to do business with one day. Introductions can be described as "unqualified leads".

Referral

The opportunity to meet someone who has an identified need for your product or service at that time. Referrals are described as "pre-qualified prospects".

Of the fifty people that I was introduced to, not one turned into a business opportunity. Admittedly I did meet some very interesting people and I'm still in contact with some of them. However, out of the five referrals I ended up doing some sort of work with four of them.

Referrals are one of the most effective approaches to new business development.

ACTION: Who can you give a referral for today?

Secret 85: Qualify your referrals

A dragon's den style event for charity? What a mad idea! But we knew it was something we had to try, so we invited five small community charities to present to a room full of wealthy and generous guests. At the end of the evening those guests were given the opportunity to pledge donations to the presenting charities. It was a great success and has gone on to raise over £1million for community charities.

Word spread fast and soon I was inundated with requests from people working with small community charities who wanted to catch up over coffee. I quickly had to develop ways of filtering all these enquiries. It was a good problem to have, but as there was no way I could say "yes" to every request, I needed to develop a way of dealing with the increase.

To an extent I found that the solution presented itself. Requests that were from people I'd never met received more attention from me when they were made through a mutual acquaintance. Quickly, I started to think about the power of a well-made referral, and it struck me that there's plenty of scope for flexibility within the referral system.

At the heart of a referral is a transfer of trust that takes place from the referrer to the referred. Referrers are therefore wise to qualify their referral.

The first way to qualify a referral is implicitly in the method you use. I consciously consider how much I trust the person I am referring and choose an approach accordingly:

Level 1: Suggestion – Bob I would recommend that you connect with Sam

Level 2: Name – Bob do reach out to Sam and feel free to mention my name

Level 3: Email – Bob I'll email introduce you to Sam

Level 4: Meeting – Bob I'll invite you and Sam for lunch

The second way to qualify a referral is through the words you use. Personally I use words such as:

"Bob and I have just met and I think you may like to meet him also"

"Bob has been a supplier for years and has always delivered an excellent service"

"Bob is a long standing friend and I would very much like you to meet"

Given that you can qualify a referral it means that you can afford to be generous in the number of referrals you give.

If you would like to receive more referrals the most important thing you can do is to build greater trust with your network of relationships. Become more intentional about developing deeper trust with the people who can refer you and your products and services.

ACTION: As a new player, how on earth do you get past the gatekeeper? It's simple – clients meet with the people they like, know and trust or the people referred to them by people they like, know and trust. Have someone refer you today.

Secret 86: Identify referral champions

Six years ago I received a referral to a private client who engaged my services and continues to do so to this day. On a regular basis the client will telephone and explain that there is someone they would like me to meet who could benefit from my services. They then arrange a lunch at their favourite restaurant in order to introduce us. To date more than 80% of these referrals have led to new business.

People who regularly feed you referrals that lead to new business are extremely valuable. I describe these people as referral champions. If you would like to identify referral champions for your business carefully consider:

Who likes, knows and trusts me?
Who understands my products/services?
Who believes in my products/services (normally because of some first hand experience)?
Who are the people already within your network who you could ask to make referrals for you?

Years ago I purchased my first property, and the guy who organised my mortgage did such a great job I have used his services for every mortgage since. I like him, know him, trust him – we're friends. I understand what he does and believe in the quality service he offers. He helps my friends, many of whom are living in houses with mortgages arranged by him. I have become one of his referral champions.

This is the power of delivering everything you say you will and more, and being likeable and trustworthy.

People will want to refer you to others.

ACTION: If you want to understand how referrals work, if you want your own business to benefit from referrals, I would recommend you become a referral champion. Consider the people who have done great work for you and start to refer them and their services to other people you know.

Secret 87: Honour referral etiquette

In every culture and every walk of life there are social norms of behaviour. Learn to adopt them and you will find it far easier to get on. And the world of referrals is no different.

At the centre of referral etiquette is a commitment to keeping your referrer in the picture. There are many good reasons for this including:

Common courtesy: this is simply a matter of good manners.

Reference request: at some point it is possible your referrer may be asked informally or formerly to give a reference for you and your work.

Repeat referral: if the referral process works well and all three parties are left with a feel good factor then hopefully there will be further referrals.

Thank you: if the referral results in you securing work then a thank you and sometimes a fee, commission or gift is appropriate.

If you follow referral etiquette and look after your referral relationships they will become increasingly confident in making referrals to you.

You will be growing referral champions who will regularly make high quality referrals for you and your business.

ACTION: Are there any reciprocal referrals that you need to make? Deal with them today.

Becoming an exceptional trusted adviser

Secret 88: Be a niche expert in a niche market

The House of Commons meeting room was packed for the launch of a cross-party report. The occasion had drawn MPs and Lords from across the parties as well as journalists, funders and business executives. At the front of the room was a table and five chairs behind which sat a panel of subject matter experts chaired by a senior Member of Parliament. I was tucked in on the end of a row towards the back of the room. Initial presentations were made and now questions were being put to the panel. In the middle of the discussion the MP chairing paused and said, 'That sounds like a question for Matt Bird!' After the initial shock and breathlessness I stood up and made some off the cuff points which I thought were rather clumsy but which met with a very warm reception.

The benefit of being known as a niche expert is that people come to you to ask for advice rather than you going to them offering your wisdom. Perhaps I am too quintessentially British, but "push marketing" – where you proactively promote your product or service to your target market – seems to be of limited value to me. Instead I prefer "pull marketing", where you focus on building your personal and organisational brand and people come to you as the niche expert. This is the dream for exceptional trusted advisers.

Becoming a niche expert requires you to focus on both a niche subject matter and a niche market. The mass market is a myth, you cannot be all things to all people. Anyone that has ever achieved significant success has done so by becoming a niche expert in a niche market. There are three steps to becoming one:

Step 1

Determine your niche expertise and niche market.

Step 2

Absorb yourself (through books, journals, blogs, conferences, thought leaders, mentors, peer relationships) in your niche expertise and market.

Step 3

Become known for being a niche expert by building your brand in your niche market. I'll come onto how you achieve this.

As an exceptional trusted adviser with niche expertise it is important that your confidence is focused on who you are rather than what you know.

If your personal confidence is based on your knowledge there is a danger you will say too much rather than listen, miss the most important things your client says and even come across as arrogant. Trust is primarily emotional and relational rather than intellectual and rational so it cannot be based solely upon your specialist knowledge but on your unique relationships. So stay human and listen even if you think you know the answer.

ACTION: Where are you at on the journey to being a niche expert? Which of the three steps above do you need to spend some time on this week?

Secret 89: Build exceptional relationships

Over twenty years ago I was on a Mediterranean holiday and met a guy called John. We talked, hit it off and became friends in an instant. Unlike many holiday friendships we actually did keep in contact. We went back packing, attended one another's weddings, celebrated achievements and supported each other in tough times. We don't see each other that often but when we do we start off exactly where we left off. I'm sure you can tell similar stories about some of your relationships.

In business I avoid using the "F" word – "Friends" – because it polarises people. For some people "friends" is a sacred category of relationship that is saved for their one or two nearest and dearest personal and private relationships. For others they have lots of "friends" and are indiscriminate about whether it is a friendship at work or at play. Personally I am a fan of making "fast friends" – and my wife often laughs at me when I describe someone I've met once or twice as a friend, but for me it is entirely normal.

Exceptional trusted advisers have the capacity and propensity to build strong relationships swiftly with a variety of clients:

Easy Relationships

There is instant relational chemistry and empathy with a person and it is easy to act for them as a professional trusted adviser.

Clunky Relationships

There is a relational connection but things are a little clunky and need a bit of TLC to get underway in order to act for them as a trusted adviser.

Challenging Relationships

There is relational disconnectedness so you are going to need to invest some blood, sweat and tears to get this professional adviser thing to work.

Exceptional trusted advisers have the relational intelligence to be able to build a client relationship relatively quickly in any one of these scenarios. Those trusted advisers who cannot do this limit themselves to building client relationships with the same kind of person – normally people like themselves.

The best trusted advisers also have the relational agility to be able to pick up relationships where they left off.

Client relationships can be seasonal, experiencing times when a relationship may be intense and other times when there is occasional contact.

Some clients only want to talk business, to get the job done and go home. Come to that, so do some trusted advisers. There is a breed of adviser who doesn't want to mix business and pleasure, and another breed of adviser who has a more blended view of life. As always what really matters here is actually the client preference and not that of the adviser. If the client wants a purely transactional relationship then so be it. Personally I believe that there is a stronger client adviser relationship if business and private lives are talked about. If both parties are able to bring their whole selves to work then the trusted adviser can advise the client in all matters.

ACTION: How well do you know your colleagues and clients? Do a mental audit of who likes to be treated in what way.

Secret 90: Anticipate client need

It was lunch time and I was meeting a client for a bite to eat. Having sat at the table and perused the menu, the waiter took our order for food. 'Thank you Mr Bird,' he said. Now, you have to understand I have been going to this restaurant since it opened twelve years ago and so the staff know me well and always call me "Mr Bird". However what surprised me was that I had never met this waiter before. A question spontaneously popped out. 'How do you know I'm Mr Bird?' The waiter rather sheepishly explained that on the wall in the kitchen there were photos of all their most frequent customers who they were asked to memorise!

I love it when businesses work to meet their customers' needs, and just as a good maitre d' will anticipate the needs of customers, so an exceptional trusted adviser will anticipate the needs of their clients. You can create the time and space to think for your client. This requires a lowering of your self-orientation (which is the tendency to view the world as about you) and instead see the world as about your client. In that place you can still your mind, suspend self-instruction, be completely present in the moment and engage in:

Heightened listening – What do I hear and not hear?
Watching and observing – What do I notice?
Following intuition – What is my gut telling me?
Scenario planning – What is the best and the worst that could happen?
Thinking big – What could we do that has never been done before?

Listening is not limited solely to the auditory.

Listening is multi sensory skill (see Secret 4) that is perhaps the most powerful competence that an exceptional trusted adviser can possess and perfect.

ACTION: Whose needs can you anticipate today?

Secret 91: Have a perspective and take risks

Recently I was approached by an organisation with a brief for a piece of work. The organisation was one of the largest within its sector, so the opportunity of working with them should have been profoundly exciting.

However, as I read through the brief I felt a little troubled. I became convinced that what they were asking for was not what they needed, so I decided to take a risk. At the pitch meeting I introduced myself and explained my perspective and told them how I thought they were looking for the wrong thing. I waited in trepidation... the client team began asking questions and I ended up spending twice as much time with them as anticipated. At the end of the session they made it very clear they wanted to work with me. I only wish I took risks more often.

Exceptional trusted advisers take risks in their relationships, while the average trusted adviser prefers to play it safe. The boldness and courage to say what the client has not thought of, or may not want to hear, is the difference between being outstanding and blending in with the crowd.

There are a multitude of ways that an exceptional trusted adviser like you can take risks with your clients:

Offering an alternative point of view
Providing candid feedback
Challenging something within the business
Sharing something personal
Acknowledging uncomfortable situations out loud

Articulating your emotions
Taking responsibility for mistakes

Taking risks requires you to trust your instinct despite the presence of uncertainty.

As one ancient proverb says, trust… 'is to be certain of what you hope for and certain of what you cannot see'. Risk is the currency of trust, and trust without risk is not trust.

ACTION: How well acquainted with risk and trust are you?

Secret 92: Build personal reputation

Day in, day out, we are bombarded with images and messages advertising products and services. There is no escape, whether surfing the Internet, watching TV, listening to the radio, reading a newspaper or magazine, driving past a billboard or travelling on the tube. Advertisers are trying to influence us by telling us what to think about their product.

Yet the difference between advertising and reputation is substantial; advertising is what we say about ourselves while reputation is what others say about us. And while we have a choice whether to advertise or not, none of us can avoid having a reputation. It's simply part and parcel of being known.

Exceptional trusted advisers are very intentional about building, managing and protecting their professional reputation and brand. It takes time to shape what people think and say about you, so you need to play the long game. Put it another way, if people are going to change what they think and say about you, they need to have a consistently different experience of you to that which they thought they would have.

The journey towards a better personal reputation takes time, so you need to be patient. However, you can influence, shape and build personal reputation in a number of ways:

Building a personal network of people who like, know and trust you.

Adding value (delivering over and above what is expected

and contracted with your clients).

Giving people a human experience of you, such as being honest about a mistake or open about your family.

Speaking and making presentations to audiences (whatever their size).

Publishing articles in magazines and journals whenever the opportunities emerge.

Blogging regularly on your niche expertise.

Engaging through a social media platform such as Twitter.

Joining a LinkedIn group on your niche expertise (if there isn't one, start one).

Asking members of your personal network if they would be willing to make referrals for you (perhaps predicated by making referrals for them).

Focusing on the ongoing, forming and strengthening your character.

The single greatest influence on your reputation is your personal character.

Abraham Lincoln once said, 'Character is like a tree and reputation like a shadow. The shadow is what we think of it; the tree is the real thing'. If your reputation becomes stronger than your character then there is a danger that you will crumble. So build reputation but remember to work on your character too.

ACTION: How much character is there behind your reputation?

Growing team relationships

Secret 93: People never really change

I've been married for over a decade, but it was not that long ago that my wife said – with a combination of complete resignation and utter relief – 'I've given up, I'm not going to be able to change you!'

None of us can change other people, whether in a marriage, friendship or business relationship. Eventually, all people who set out to change others will reach a point of resignation. The first question that every team should ask themselves is:

How do you get people to do what you want?

There are a range of ways that people try to get people to do what they want to do: tell them, persuade them, influence them, suggest to them, listen to them. The reality is that most people don't like being told what to do, so the "tell them" approach rarely works. By contrast the "listen to them" approach can create incredible understanding and openness. However, it remains very difficult to get people to do what you want them to do.

The best answer to our question is this; you can't. You get the best out of people when you encourage them to do what they want to do. This is what I call playing to strength. Talent is defined as any recurring pattern of thought, feeling, or behaviour that can be productively applied to become a strength. You can help identify your talent by asking:

What can you not help but do?
What can you do easily and virtually without trying?
What do you desire to do?
What do you learn fast?
What satisfies you?

The best thing you can ask of your team is for people to be the best possible version of themselves. Similarly, the best thing that you can do for your team is to be the best possible version of yourself.

ACTION: Think about the people you work with. What talents do they have that can be developed into a strength. It may even be that roles can be redesigned to make more of talent and strength. How do you help people in your team do more of what they are good at every day?

Secret 94: Master compromise

Two friends are out for drinks and one likes red wine and the other likes white. What bottle of wine do they order? A family has a movie night and one child wants to watch a Pixar film and another child wants to watch a DreamWorks' film, Which do they watch? The neighbourhood committee can't agree on which of two dates for the annual street party, which do they choose? A business is launching a new product and is divided on two different routes to market – which is adopted?

Life and relationships are full of differences of opinion, apparent contradictions and potential compromises. I am not talking about a compromise of values of right and wrong. I am talking about a compromise of preference of living life my way. The second question that every team should ask themselves is:

How often do you compromise?

Never

You are used to having your own way. Your selfishness and rigidity is probably causing frustration and annoyance to the people around you.

Frequently

You are self-aware and self-confident. You know what makes relationships thrive and flourish, and that includes the ability to compromise.

Always

The people around you could be taking advantage of you. You may need to learn to speak up for yourself and be a little more assertive in expressing your preferences.

Compromise is to relationships what breathing is to life. Compromise is a requirement of every relationship whether in the life of a family, community or workplace. Room needs to be made for each family member, neighbour, colleague, supplier and client so that they feel included and at home. The capacity to be attentive and adaptable in this way is what I describe as relational intelligence.

ACTION: What do you need to compromise on at the moment? What would your colleagues, your boss or your partner say?

Secret 95: Commit to a results orientation

There were twenty of us sat around the board table for a charity committee. We had been in the meeting for two hours and I can't quite remember when I had slipped into the semi-comatose state that I eventually found myself in. For a while a good friend and I had entertained ourselves by texting each other across the table. Now I was counting the minutes, and there was still an hour to go. Why on earth were we meeting as a team?

There are some useful things to do when you meet as a team and there are also some things that could be wasting everyone's time and breath. The third question that every team should ask themselves is:

Why does your team meet?

Not so great reasons could be:
    To give and receive reports
    To watch powerpoint slides
    To update one another
    To do so because that's what is in the diary

Great reasons could be:
    To solve problems
    To innovate
    To discuss strategy
    To brainstorm ideas
    To improve performance

I once remember hearing a talk from a senior executive about the three great attributes of a leader. Of the three attributes the one that has stuck in my mind, when the others have been long forgotten is "results orientation". This seems particularly pertinent to the leadership of team meetings. What is the point? Why are we meeting? What is the outcome? If this question can't be answered clearly, concisely and convincingly then perhaps you shouldn't be meeting. Why does your team meet?

ACTION: The next time you're in a meeting, ask 'Why?' How can you behave in ways to fully maximise the meeting's potential?

Secret 96: With and without you

Kim was appointed to lead the learning and development function of a blue chip professional services business. On joining, Kim undertook a review of the role and purpose of the team. It was clear in the mind of the team that their role and purpose was to provide training opportunities to people within the business. It was not clear how this drove business objectives.

So the team began to review the entire business value chain in order to understand how they were responsible for driving the business forward. Then all became clear; the role and purpose of the team was "to help our people be confident with our clients".

It is surprisingly easy for a team to be very busy doing what it should be doing but not knowing why. Teams benefit from knowing why what they are doing is driving the business. The fifth question that every team should ask themselves is:

What does your organisation look like with and without your team?

If the answer is:

> No difference

> The team is under performing and a major review of how the team plays its part in driving business success is required.

Small difference

The team is performing but needs to recalibrate itself so it is unquestionably adding value to driving business success.

Significant difference

The team is peak performing and no immediate change is needed – whilst recognising that such a team will continue to push itself.

Every team should be making a quantifiable and measurable contribution to the businesses value chain. If there is little or no value added then there needs to be swift and effective change.

ACTION: What does your organisation look like with and without your team?

Benefiting from business relationships

Secret 97: Personal prosperity

In the early years of our careers the focus is on becoming technically excellent in our chosen craft. The further we progress in our careers, the more we begin to realise that our technical ability is assumed. If we were technically deficient or unable to grasp new skills swiftly we would no longer be in the job. At this point some people hit one of life's glass ceilings until they realise that their future career progress is no longer based upon their technical excellence but upon their ability to get on with people.

The Dale Carnegie Institute has undertaken research studies in multiple industries which demonstrate that 'about 15% of financial success is due to technical knowledge and 85% is due to skill in human engineering.'

Your career may have got underway on the basis of your education, qualifications and intellect, but whether you reach the top will largely depend upon your relationology. Just how well do you get on with, read and respond to people? To what level have you developed your leadership, influencing and negotiating skills? Remember the way on in your career will not be the same as the way into your career.

So no matter what IQ you have been given, if you want to succeed in your chosen vocation, work at developing your

EQ (Emotional Intelligence). Intentionally develop, practice and master your:

Self-awareness
Social awareness
Self-mastery
Social mastery

The quality of your interpersonal relationships is possibly the greatest determinate of your vocational success and personal prosperity.

Maybe it's a little crass, but the saying "Your network determines your net worth" does at least highlight this important truth.

ACTION: The first business benefit of relationships is personal prosperity. What could you do this week to make an investment in the development of your emotional intelligence?

Secret 98: New Business

It's been below freezing most nights for a week and suddenly your boiler stops working. The car has started making an unusual noise that sounds terminal and threatens to spoil your plans to go away next weekend. You have recently moved house and need to find a babysitter to look after the kids while you and your wife go out on a much-needed night out. Where are you going to turn? Are you going to trust some directory to signpost you to a boiler engineer, car mechanic or child minding service?

People prefer to do business with people they know and trust rather than people they don't. It is built into our human nature. But how do we find the people who will become long-term features of our life? This is when it comes down to three factors:

Personal recommendation of someone you know and trust.

Professional referral from another supplier you know and trust (it is not worth the risk of them suggesting someone they couldn't bank on).

"Word of mouth" reputation through someone you know and trust.

It takes time and care to build relationships and reputation, however once established they become invaluable to winning new business. So much new business development relies on old fashioned direct mail and cold calling, which is increasingly ineffective. I was amused recently to see a job advert for a head of New Business Development which was described as "Urgent". My view is that if it was urgent it was too late!

If you need an accountant for a large business you may consider the big four professional services firms. However, from the outside they all look pretty much the same. So you are likely to choose an accountant from within a firm where you know and trust somebody.

Relationships offer the ultimate differentiator and competitive advantage.

In fact, I'd like to take it one step further. You are probably willing to pay more to work with somebody you know and trust rather than somebody you don't. Knowledge and trust is commercially valuable.

ACTION: The second business benefit of relationships is new business. What sort of relationship do you have and do you aspire to have, with your clients and prospective clients?

Secret 99: Employee engagement

How many times in a week do you get a phone call at work from someone who doesn't want something from you? It is likely that you can probably count the number of those phone calls on one hand. Sometimes it seems that every phone call and every email makes another demand on you. In our working environment there is a danger that every human interaction becomes transactional. This may appear to get the tasks completed in the short term, however in the long term it will build a transactional culture with low levels of trust.

When I was a local government councillor I regularly picked a road in my community and spent a couple of hours on a Saturday morning knocking on doors to meet the people I represented and find out more about the needs of the local community. Having introduced myself I was often asked by people when the next local election was scheduled. They all assumed that I was at their door canvassing for their vote. When I explained that there was no local election due I'd often get a look of astonishment.

Sometimes it is the little things that make the biggest difference to how people feel engaged in the organisation. Today and in the coming week, why don't you reach out in non-transactional ways to build relationships.

Could you telephone or email (if you have to) a colleague just to see how they are doing? How about meeting with someone for a coffee without having an agenda or favour to ask? Why not contact someone in your organisation who is working at another site or in another country just to catch up?

There is incredible power in building non-transactional interactions with people.

When people begin to realise you are there for them and not just for what you can get from them, a far stronger relationship is established. However, the pressure for businesses to perform leads to a greater focus on the financial bottom line, which in turn drives towards a transactional and dehumanising culture. So this is the challenge – how do you build a culture that respects, trusts and engages people in economically stressed times?

ACTION: The third business benefit of relationships is employee engagement. What could you do to build greater trust amongst your colleagues this week?

Secret 100: Efficiency and effectiveness

Just last week I popped into a branch of my bank to make an enquiry. I spoke to the cashier who said I needed to speak to a business manager who in turn advised me that I needed to speak to my own business manager. The following day I phoned their office, only to find out that they were on a course. So I spoke to the business manager who was standing in. I was informed that I should telephone the following day to speak to my personal business manager. When I eventually spoke to my personal business manager they recommended I telephone the call centre!

Sometimes our organisations create systems and procedures in the name of efficiency and effectiveness but they are everything but that.

You may have promised yourself recently to be more efficient and effective with your time. You may be trying to adopt a new way of working to improve your personal performance and squeeze every last ounce out of life, such as:

Learning how to use new Project Management software to enable you to plan and schedule every stage of your assignments.

Hiring a Personal Assistant or if you have one of those, perhaps a Diary Secretary to help manage your life and work.

Using the Customer Relationship Management system your organisation invested in but you have never used.

You can adopt all the systems and structures your

organisation has to offer, however nothing can improve your personal efficiency and effectiveness like trust. In fact, excessive policies and procedures create a culture that communicates "you are not trusted".

The easiest, fastest and cheapest way to get anything done is through trusting relationships.

Relationships will always produce the highest levels of performance and profitability. When you need a fast turnaround or you need something doing in a certain way, you will turn to people you know and trust.

ACTION: The fourth business benefit of relationships is efficiency and effectiveness. What are you doing to build a culture of trust and loyalty within your organisation?

Secret 101: Growth and profitability

It was an unexpected telephone call and an unusual request that Monday morning. An invitation from one of the big four professional services firms to be their guest speaker at an annual service they were hosting at one of London's Cathedrals. I always relish a new challenge, the date worked, so of course I accepted.

In the middle of my speech I mentioned the organisation's vision, which states that it "does the right thing for our clients, colleagues and community". Now, why on earth would a commercial organisation place such an emphasis on right relationships?

It's simple; good relationships lead to good business and bad relationships lead to bad business.

The Service-Profit Chain developed by a group of professors from Harvard Business School provides a more sophisticated answer – it demonstrates the causal relationships that exist between:

Employee engagement
Employee satisfaction and loyalty
Customer satisfaction and loyalty
Business growth and profitability

Even without the authority of one of the world's top business schools it makes sense. People and relationships matter and they matter more than anything else.

There are many factors that lead to the fracturing of relationships and therefore the breakdown of trust in the Service-Profit Chain including frequent restructuring, high employee turnover and a "blame" culture. What are the things in your organisation that make building strong relationships more difficult?

The aspects of business that we have been told are "soft" actually turn out to be the "hard" stuff of business. People in quality relationships drive and determine the bottom line of every business. And that's the fifth business benefit of relationships – growth and profitability.

ACTION: What are you doing this week to build stronger relationships in your value chain?

About Matt

Matt Bird helps people and organisations build the relationships they need to achieve greater success. He has created Relationology: the art and science of relationships and how they drive life significance and business success.

He is an international keynote speaker and consultant who inspires people to believe they can and imparts insights to enable them to succeed. His programmes are renowned for creating lasting change. He specialises working in professional services on new business development and client relationship management.

Matt is an award winning author, magazine columnist and popular blogger whose business relationship insights are read globally by thousands of leaders every week www.relationology.co.uk

> 'When Malcolm Gladwell sat at his typewriter and wrote the chapter on connectors in The Tipping Point, he must have just finished a slap-up lunch with Matt Bird.'
> **Campaign Magazine**

Matt is also the founder of The Cinnamon Network which helps address social breakdown by building relational capital in communities. As a philanthropist he has raised millions for good causes including through his Dragon's Den style events for charity. His charitable work has received commendations from successive British Governments and Prime Ministers.

> *'I'm pleased to be able to give The Cinnamon Network this Big Society Award in recognition of the huge difference they have made across the country.'*
> **Prime Minister David Cameron**

Matt lives in London, UK with his wife Esther and their three children.

www.relationology.co.uk
mattbird@relationology.co.uk

Acknowledgements

Relationology has benefitted from the help and generosity of many people whom I want to say a "thank you".

A very special thanks to my patient and enduring wife, Esther.

Thank you to the people whose friendship and example never fails to inspire me: Lyndon Bowring, Wayne Malcolm, Mike Royal, David Westlake, Laurence Singlehurst, Jeremy Higham, John Glen, Shane Mullins and Charlie Boyle.

Thanks also to Rob Parsons for helping shape this project, Ricky Kalsi for your constant advice, Craig Borlase for his masterful help with the edit, Rich Ward for the brilliant cover and Heather Townsend for all our conversations over the title and much more.